Find the Good

Also by Heather Lende

Take Good Care of the Garden and the Dogs

If You Lived Here, I'd Know Your Name

Find
the
Good

Unexpected Life Lessons from

a Small-Town Obituary Writer

Heather Lende

ALGONQUIN BOOKS OF CHAPEL HILL   2015

Published by

ALGONQUIN BOOKS OF CHAPEL HILL

Post Office Box 2225

Chapel Hill, North Carolina 27515-2225

a division of

WORKMAN PUBLISHING

225 Varick Street

New York, New York 10014

Library of Congress Cataloging-in-Publication Data

Lende, Heather, [date]

Find the good / by Heather Lende.

pages cm

ISBN 978-1-61620-167-8

1. Attitude (Psychology) 2. Conduct of life.

I. Title.

BF327.L46 2015

170'.44 — dc23   2014038663

10 9 8 7 6 5 4 3

For Caroline Cooper, Lani, Ivy,
Silvia Rose, and James,
with love.

∾

Contents

Find the Good

The Good News

Recently, I was asked to write a short essay describing one piece of wisdom to live by. I thought about it but did not have a brief, easy answer. I have made enough mistakes in my life to fill a whole bookshelf of dos and don'ts. My friend John works as an investigator in the public defender's office but is a poet. That is probably why he managed to distill all his fatherly hopes and dreams into two rules for his only child: "Be nice to the dog and don't do meth." His son turned out kind, clear-eyed, and he graduated from a good college.

I didn't have such pithy haiku wisdom at the ready. As an obituary writer, I lean toward elegiac couplets, and I have five children, which also adds a lot more variables. One size won't fit all of them. I took another tack. I pretended I was on my deathbed. (I'm fifty-four, have survived being run over by a truck, and I had a headache, which I worried might be a brain tumor, so this was not such a big leap.) I imagined I'd already said good-bye to my husband, children, grandchildren, and all the great-grandchildren I hadn't even met yet. If indeed all the wisdom I had in my heart was to be summed up in final words and it was difficult to speak more than, say, three, what would I rasp before my soul flew up the chimney?

Find the good.

I surprised myself with this pretty great notion.

Find the good. That's enough. That's plenty. I could leave my family with that.

My "beat" at our local newspaper is death, which is why I was asked to contribute the essay in the first place. Since I have written obituaries in Haines, Alaska (pop. about 2,000), the town where I live, for almost twenty years, the journal's editor assumed that I must know something about last words and good lives. (After all, it is wrong to speak ill of the dead.) Turns out that I do. It just took me a while to believe it, and even longer to say it out loud.

Writing obituaries is my way of transcending bad news. It has taught me the value of intentionally trying to find the good in people and situations, and that practice—and I do believe that finding the good can be practiced—has made my life more meaningful. I begin each obituary with a phone conversation, followed by a visit. For reasons I'm not sure of, but that one priest told me may be my calling, I am able to enter a grieving household, pull up a chair, sip some coffee, observe, listen, ask questions that (I hope) will ease the pain, take notes, and recognize the authentic lines when I hear them. Finding the good in this situation is often challenging; it is not always obvious. If I concentrate and am patient, though, it will reveal itself. This usually involves a lot of caffeine.

After an elder who has been housebound and incapacitated by a stroke for twenty-five years dies, I find time to sit on the sofa and look through family albums with his widow and admire how handsome he was in his World War II uniform and how happy they both looked on that beach vacation the year before he was stricken.

When twelve-year-old twins lose their mother to cancer, I will quote their father praising them and tell how he plans to take them on a family drive across the country to see their grandparents.

And perhaps hardest of all, on the snowy winter morning when I meet with the parents and siblings of a young man who drank too much one night and shot himself, I write down how very much he had loved to swim in the lake in front of their summer cabin.

I understand why you may think that what I do is depressing, but compared to front-page news, most obituaries are downright inspirational. People lead all kinds of interesting and fulfilling lives, but they all end. My task is investigating the deeds, characteristics, occupations, and commitments, all that he or she made of their "one wild and precious life," as poet Mary Oliver has called it. He may have died mumbling and confused in a nursing home, but in his day he was a fine actor, dashing host, and bon vivant you would have loved playing charades with. She was a terrific big sister, the daughter who always baked cookies for her dad, and had planned on attending an art college before she was killed in a car wreck. No one wants the last hour of her life to eclipse the seventeen years before it.

Compared to most front-page news the obituaries are downright inspirational.

This may not be how the obituary writers at national newspapers work, but I'm dealing with people I know—my neighbors in the small, close-knit community where my husband owns a lumberyard, where we've raised our family, where I've sat on the school board, volunteer for hospice, and am a regular at the Morning Muscles exercise class. These relationships alter the way I write. Before I compose an obituary, I ask myself what truths will outlive the facts of this person's life, what needs to be in it but also what doesn't.

Tom Morphet, my editor at the *Chilkat Valley News,* often disagrees with my choices and asks me to dig a little deeper into the more difficult times in a person's life. He warns me against habitually walking on the sunny side of the street.

Still, I leaned close to the radio recently when I heard a story about a study that proved optimistic women live longer. I called Tom right up with the great news.

"At least you believe you will," he replied.

Tom and I were both pleased with the way the obituary of an old miner unfolded. His widow and daughters wanted to be sure I included the bad with the good. Rather than detour around his sinkholes, they told me to note that he had been a hard-drinking, hard-living, and some would even say hard-hearted, man who was transformed by a voice he heard in a blizzard while driving through a mountain pass, telling him to change his ways. He did, becoming a sober, tender, nursery-rhyme singer as soon as his first grandbaby gripped his finger. He taught all his grandchildren to sing along when he played the guitar. If grandchildren can help an old miner find the Lord on his rough road to Damascus, what am I going to discover thanks to mine?

I think about children first when bad things happen. How can we reaffirm that there's so much to applaud, even if they see nothing worthy of an ovation? And then I know. Whenever there is a tragedy, from the horrific school shooting in Newtown, Connecticut, to when a fisherman dies after slipping off the deck here in Haines, awful events are followed by dozens and dozens of good deeds. It's not that misery loves company, exactly; rather, it's that suffering, in all its forms, and our response to it, binds us together across dinner tables, neighborhoods, towns and cities, and even time. Bad doings bring out the best in people.

Lives were saved at the finish line of the Boston Marathon because bystanders ran toward the explosions to help, rather than away from them. This is what Fred "Mr." Rogers's mother wanted him to notice when he was frightened by scary news. "Look for the helpers," she told him. "You will always find people helping." Mr. Rogers passed along that advice to millions of other children (and their parents) who were scared or angered by violence or tragedy, and it helped them, too.

Look for the EMTs wheeling the stretcher into the ambulance.

Look for the guys grilling hot dogs for hurricane refugees.

Look for the motorcycle club collecting canned goods for the food bank.

~∞~

SLY STONE SANG IT LOUD. *We are family*. Our hearts are every bit as malleable as stardust turned to gold. Loving one another polishes them.

"Where do stars come from?" my oldest granddaughter, Caroline, asked one winter evening when her parents were out and I was tucking her into bed. I told her, and she wondered why we only see them when the sun goes down. Darkness makes light visible, I explained, echoing Emerson. I didn't say that I imagine stars represent the people who used to live with us and aren't here anymore, and how perfect it is that they twinkle rather than glare hotly down on us, and maybe that's why they call the night sky the heavens. That would be even further over her head.

After Goldilocks ran off, we dimmed the bedside lamp and whispered about bears, what porridge is, and why walking into other people's houses when they are not home is a bad idea. Then Caroline pointed out the window again. "I love the stars," she said and stuttered the way she does because her thoughts are faster than her tongue. "I really, really, love, love stars, don't you Mi-Mimi?" (She gave me the new name to go with my new role.)

This afternoon I will finish that short essay on finding the good and then walk on the beach with my granddaughters. I'll look for heart-shaped rocks while little Caroline and toddling Lani and Ivy tumble behind me, dumping sand from one pail to the other, stomping in tide pools and climbing over driftwood. You probably wouldn't know the gray gravel is littered with hearts unless someone showed you, but once you do, you can find lots of them.

Sometimes, I set down these found hearts on top of logs for passersby to notice. Other times I fill my pockets with them. I gave one to my husband on Valentine's Day. There are three on the kitchen windowsill, one on my dresser. Lani and Ivy are still too young to know what they are, but Caroline, at three and a half, finds sand-smoothed baby-palm-sized hearts all over our house. I have taught her to watch for them on our beach walks, too. Some days there are more than others.

When Caroline asks if she can take my current favorite heart rock home, I say yes. I have faith that there are plenty more where it came from and that we will find them.

Pretty Good Is
Better Than Perfect

It is early summer, which means our house is full. My son is back for the season to fish commercially, my two daughters who teach school in Juneau are in Haines for the week, and the other two, who live here with their young families, are downstairs with my dad, who is in town for his annual visit from New York. I had the place all polished and tidied up for their arrival, but now it looks like the tail end of a three-family rummage sale.

My "office" is on the landing of our staircase and I'm trying to finish an obituary. It's just about done, but I can't help hearing everyone talking at once, babies and toddlers crying and laughing, and an occasional growl and yip and "stop it." Sarah brought her baying part-bloodhound with her, and Eliza's energetic puppy, Annie (whom my oldest granddaughter thinks is named "Stop It"), came up on the ferry from Juneau, too. Both dogs are wrestling with Pearl, our young golden retriever. My daughters are teasing my dad, who is trying to call New York on a cell phone even though we don't have reception here on a clear day, let alone this stormy one. Over the din, my son is playing the guitar and singing something about wishing he'd known then what he knows now.

The weather has chased everybody indoors. They have adapted by turning the living room into a playpen. The furniture is back against the walls so the babies can crawl on the old rug that used to be in their great-great-grandmother's house. The books have been pulled from the bottom shelves and the dining chairs are lying down, fencing off the hot woodstove. My daughter lit it to take the dampness out of the air. When I walk through to get another cup of coffee, I step over blocks and crayons. A deck of cards and chips from an open bag are scattered across the coffee table; there is dog hair all over the babies' knees.

I really ought to vacuum. I should. But the only thing I pick up off the floor is a baby clinging to my pants. Brushing the fur and sand off her legs, I hold her close enough to feel her heart beating. Listening to the words my son is singing, I realize that I actually do know a couple of things now that I didn't know when I was younger, and I'm so glad I acted on them as I happily survey the pretty good remodel of my once-perfect home.

ell

I SPENT A GOOD CHUNK of my life trying to be the perfect daughter, perfect student, perfect bride, perfect mother, perfect friend, perfect wife—not to mention keeping a perfect house, serving perfect meals, and tending perfect chickens who laid perfect eggs. In any free hours, I ran a lot. A year after I had my fourth baby, I completed my first marathon.

By the time my fifth child arrived, though, I had begun rethinking "perfect." She was an eight-year-old Bulgarian orphan who was every bit as "perfect" a daughter as the biological children I had fretted over. Among many other things, she taught us all the value of positive thinking. About the time Stoli joined our family, I began to notice that the obituaries that resonated with me most were ones about flawed people—I hate to say "imperfect" now that I have turned that notion on its head—who had different priorities than say, Eagle Scouts, yet were praised by friends and acquaintances alike for their generosity, their sense of humor, or, possibly, a hidden talent.

Like Shane, the waitress who wanted to be a painter but instead satisfied her creative spirit by arranging hamburgers and French fries artfully. She was eulogized for her attention to that eye-pleasing detail. "Her plates always looked beautiful," her boss Christy told me, adding that Shane and the rest of the crew at the Pioneer Bar and adjacent grill were like a convivially dysfunctional family. "Shane was one of those people I fired about five times, but she was a great person. I loved her. She was smart and funny." Christy said she hired Shane more than she fired her, and when I suggested that seemed kind of crazy, she explained how managing a bar is difficult and staffing one even more so, but that has forced her to appreciate the good in people and forgive, and sometimes ignore, the bad. "Otherwise, what's the point?"

Or Art Jess, an eighty-three-year-old elder who many in town considered a sage. The Native American leader was generous, wise, and an articulate and compelling speaker who was active in community organizations, from the American Legion and the library to the Haines People for Peace and the Northern Tide Dancing and Drumming Circle. Above all, Art was an extraordinary listener. He paid attention and remembered what people said to him. That's rare.

Speaking with his wife while researching his life, I

learned that Art was born severely dyslexic. Reading was hard for him and he could not write a word. Because of his disability he became a skilled listener, his mind absorbing everything like a sponge and remembering it all. Art's greatest talent was born out of necessity, thanks to what some would call an imperfection in his very good brain.

The reverse of that silver lining is that making everything "just so" can be a hindrance to living your best life. The obituary I wrote where the highest praise anyone could offer about the woman was, "She kept her stove clean," worried me. True, it was a huge black-and-nickel antique wood-burning cookstove, but still. At least she never read that.

Not long after writing that obituary, I was invited to dinner at a new friend's rental house, which was equipped with a rusting gas stove. We assembled homemade tamales on our laps while sitting on stools in the drafty old kitchen. It was one of the nicest evenings in one of the warmest (yet least so-called perfect) homes I've ever been in. My host did not, as I would have at the time, iron the napkins. He passed around a roll of paper towels that doubled as plates.

Sure, I knew all along that no one ever demanded perfection in my household except me. I thought it was my job to keep it orderly and clean. I am good at that. Sometimes it's easier to scrub the shower stall than have that heart-to-heart talk with your teenage daughter about the boyfriend you believe is not nice to her. Rather than keep on keeping on, living as I'd always done, it was time to make a few changes. I knew it wouldn't occur overnight or even in a few weeks. Change is a process.

But that's okay, better actually, and healthier than viewing the decades (hopefully) remaining as a highly perishable product with an expiration date. I have a friend who says we spend the first half of our life building it and the second half preventing it from falling apart. I'd rather be under construction when I die. At this point, acceptance is more of a goal for me than, say, cleanliness. For some people it isn't. I have another friend who prefers to be a little grumpy but very neat, rather than cheerful and untidy. She's pretty sure these traits are inversely related. I suspect she may be right because my house is getting messier in direct proportion to my growing optimism. So the sticky fingerprints on my windows can just stay right where they are, thank you very much. The old question should not be, is the cup half full or half empty, but, what will happen when that grandchild spills it? Will I moan or refill it?

"Mimi, may I have some milk?" little Caroline asks as she watches me add a splash to my coffee. When she doesn't want to sit at the table and drink it, I say, "Then how about water instead? Will that work?" I fill the cup halfway and watch without a wince as she skips splashing away. That's what perfect looks like. Perfect, too, are the black curls on the back of the baby's head that my daughter is now nursing in the window seat, and the fishy scent of low tide when another daughter lets the dogs out, and the farewell nod of the last daffodil under the cherry tree, and the blue of a cracked mussel one of my grandchildren must have dropped from her pailful and that I just stepped on.

In *Gift from the Sea*, Anne Morrow Lindbergh wrote about relationships, motherhood, aging, and leading a meaningful life. I love the part where she talks about the way we all wear proverbial shells—the shell of ambition, the shell of accumulations and possessions, the shell of the ego—which in middle age we, like oysters and whelks, may also shed.

Now is a good time for me to toss the old shells of perfection and bother, of being in charge—"the Boss of this Place," as my children dubbed me when they were small—and grow or create, or most likely just patch to-

My house is getting messier in direct proportion to my growing optimism.

gether from shards of all the other ones, a newer, more flexible shell to carry me through the second half of my life with a little more grace and a lot more compromise.

And later this summer, as my grandchildren and I

are all getting our hands dirty in the garden and we pull that first skinny little carrot out of the soil, I will show them for sure what perfect really is, and understand deep in the compost I came from, have enriched, and will one day return to, that it's got nothing to do with me.

Stop and Smell
the Fish

I'm looking out the window, watching the tide come in at the beach behind my house, as I sit at my desk typing in my two-fingered way. I'm writing an obituary about fisherman and carpenter Norm Blank and I smile when I reread my notes about how his wife of fifty-four years said he wasn't quick to mend a hole in his net—it allowed a few more salmon to live to breed for another year. It figures that I'd be writing this just as a new fishing season has begun. Norm would have appreciated being in sync with the salmon life cycle. Maybe that's why he hung on all winter, as his pulmonary fibrosis swiftly progressed. So he could be buried near the Chilkat River in June, when the sockeye run.

His wife also told me how, when the family was growing, Norm quit a perfectly good state job that offered steady pay and retirement benefits because he was being asked to work outside of Haines. It would actually have been a promotion, but Norm wanted to have more time at home with his wife and their daughters.

Bronnie Ware, a palliative care nurse, wrote that the greatest regret of most people she cared for, especially men, was working too much when they could have been enjoying their families, but that was no doubt generational and will be much more gender neutral from now on. The other regret many dying people shared with her was not cultivating closer relationships.

One year Norm took a break from his usual off-season carpentry work, packed up the kids in a VW van, and drove across the country. When he was in his seventies, he'd stop by the café in town to collect the recycling and turn the chore into an opportunity to meet new folks or visit with old friends. (He volunteered to haul it, so his coffee was always free.) As Norm's friend told me, "He was fun to be around. We all should be so lucky to have both kids still in town, and die in our own home. What more could you wish?"

I want to be like Norm. And not just the part about nearby children and dying old in bed. Norm and his wife kept their place as inviting as any home I've ever been in. He always had a project to work on. He liked to refurbish old bikes and toys to give to needy kids. And there were those nets to mend and his special greasy-good salmon bellies to smoke. Yet he would happily greet an unexpected visitor—and not only from far away and right off the ferry, but also the neighbor from across the street—and then sit overlooking the garden and talk as if he had nothing better to do. Whenever I asked his daughter, my friend Anna, how he was able to do this so frequently, she'd laugh and say something like, "Well, he doesn't have anything better to do."

She probably thought I was as dumb as a post (though she is too nice to say so). Because anyone can see that the real answer is priorities and what's at the top of your to-do list. I bet Norm's would read like this: (1) family, (2) friends, (3) everybody else I bump into, and (4) fish, followed by all the usual items that, speaking strictly for myself, must be checked off before getting to all the fun stuff. I don't need a palliative care nurse to tell me where those intentions lead.

~ele~

My eighty-one-year-old neighbor Elizabeth says, "Growing old is the pits." And yet, while she spent about twenty Aprils on her knees yanking up dandelions by the roots and tossing them on a burn pile, now that she is unable to, she says, "If dandelions were hard to grow we'd call them flowers." She doesn't regret the time spent eradicating them; she stopped before it wore her out. I could tell you that Elizabeth has no choice but to slow down and smell the dandelions. But that's not true. She does. She could hate the sight of her yellow-carpeted lawn until the day she dies, and no one would blame her. But where is the good in that?

Just like Norm. Yes, he could do all kinds of very important things all day and not stop everything when his teenage granddaughter walks over looking for a cookie and maybe needing a hug. He could promise he'll hike to Battery Point with her three days from now, as soon as he gets another coat of varnish on the bookshelf and trims the hedge. But he'd never have done that.

Maybe it's because Norm walked a lot of years in the valley of the shadow of death. The men in his family died relatively young of a hereditary lung disease for which he carried the genetic marker as well. His good health and fitness—right up to a few months before the pulmonary fibrosis kicked in and he died—were remarkable. The positive thinker in me would like to believe that some people, and Norm would certainly be one, are born with an emotional happiness gene that overrides inherited physical flaws. I'll have to ask a doctor if that's possible. On the other hand, I'm not sure we have that much control, as any of our lives can end in a blink. In Mandarin, there is one character for heart and mind. What both halves of my heart-mind can agree on is that I am the one who chooses how to respond to the people and situations I encounter everyday. You don't have to know a guy like Norm or be an obituary writer to connect the dots and shift priorities

Cry a lot after a friend dies.
Then, when you've had all the sorrow
you can handle, take a walk
down by the river to wring yourself out.
Invite a new friend over for coffee.
Begin again.

so your regrets will be no worse than wanting one more day with the people you have loved well in the place that means the world to you.

Norm had more practice than I will in getting life right, because he figured it out sooner—way back when he met a pretty girl at an ice cream parlor and knew in that moment he'd marry her, and soon did. When he was with that young bride in traffic on the San Francisco Bridge and couldn't stand the congestion and said, "Let's go to Alaska," she said okay. Not all of us are that lucky. I will begin, not by totally flipping my to-do list upside down—that would be hard for me—but by taking advantage of a day that is topsy-turvy without my consent.

If the snow keeps me home from an important meeting, I'll take a walk in it. Shovel my neighbor's stoop. Then build a snowman at the end of the driveway. When was the last time I did that? When my plane is delayed for two hours, I'll call Dad. Listen to the entire saga of his knee replacement surgery and recovery. Ask him how he's adjusting to living alone after forty-nine years of marriage. I'll finally have the time to listen. And I'll cry a lot after a friend dies. Attend the funeral. Bring my best bean salad to the potluck. Wallow in grief. When I've had all the sorrow I can bear, I'll take a hike down by the river to wring myself out. Then

I'll be ready to invite a new friend over for coffee and begin again.

⁓

It's a beautiful day and Norm, of all people, would think me nuts for sitting inside on such a sunny afternoon. But I still need to write a sentence or two about his environmental activism, although he'd never, ever call it that. Norm's concern for the health of the planet was a natural (pardon the pun) extension of the way he prioritized all that he valued. He knew John Muir was right when he wrote that everything on earth is hitched together by the same invisible life-giving cord. Norm testified at public hearings against harmful development; served on the advisory board of the forty-thousand-acre Chilkat Bald Eagle Preserve, which he also had a hand in creating about thirty-five years ago; and helped protect the wild salmon runs on the Chilkat River, which empties into the sea in my backyard.

The very backyard where I now see my daughter and granddaughter waving to me from the beach. I open the window and say I'll be right there, and decide to keep the ending of Norm's obituary simple by quoting his friend Tim: "When it came to protecting fisheries and fish habitat, Norm always spoke on behalf of the fish."

Speak for the fish. Norm would have liked to have that be among his last words. I look over my copy one more time and know what it's telling me to do. I fix a mistake, tighten a sentence, send it off to the paper, and then run down to meet my family—with no regrets.

Draw Lines in the Sand
So You Can Move Them

A year and half ago our youngest daughter, Stoli, was pregnant, not married, and in case you're wondering, had just turned twenty-one.

There are several words in that sentence I thought I'd never utter. With four daughters and one son, I take parenting seriously. I am also acutely aware of the commitment motherhood entails. I was proactive about sex education and the dangers of unplanned pregnancies. I haven't been a member of Planned Parenthood all these years for nothing. I knew so much way back when about parenting that I wrote enough columns about it to buy the small, crumbling, thirty-year-old former summer cottage adjacent to our backyard. Chip and I intended to tear most of it down and perhaps make the remaining studio over the garage a vacation rental or our smaller house, someday. Two weeks after we closed on the place, Stoli announced the surprise pregnancy. She told her father and siblings while I was away, and they agreed Chip would break the news to me privately when I returned.

I guess no one wanted to be there when the top of my head blew off.

That didn't happen, but my heart took a bad fall. This was not what I had planned for *my* baby girl. How will she rear a child, finish school, and support herself? Just thinking about it made me manic and miserable: Oh, she is so pretty and her boyfriend is so handsome, what a beautiful baby they will make. Oh, she'll be a single mother without a college degree. Life will be so hard.

"She's happy," Chip said, pointing out that Stoli was only a year younger than I was when we got married. Her boyfriend, Nels, was a nice kid from another big local family. They'd dated for years and had gone to the high school prom together.

Chip suggested they could live next door until they were on their feet. We'd only have to fix up the cottage a little. Insulate. Paint. Replace broken windows. Do something about the smell. "We can rip up the moldy carpeting, and at least the woodstove is still in good shape," he said, also admitting that the place might need an additional oil heater in the back room. Nels could help with the work.

When I said that was actually *a lot* and sputtered that our plans had been ruined, Chip said, "I don't know about you, but I can think of nothing better than having another grandchild running across the yard to visit us." At the time, Stoli's older sister Sarah's toddler, Caroline, was our only granddaughter. I never anticipated loving her so fiercely.

Chip said, "You want to know what would worry

me more than an unwed pregnant daughter? If she moved to New Jersey. What would we do if she were all the way out there? Even if they were married that would be terrible."

All I heard was "married."

Of course marriage is not the answer to everyone's happiness, even if it has been for me. I read the news. I know that at best there's a fifty-fifty success rate. I even hated the way my own voice sounded when I suggested a wedding would solve everything. But what was a good mother to do?

"Nothing," Chip said. "We're doing enough working on the house. Stop trying to fix something that isn't broken. It's not like she's in the hospital with a terminal illness. It's a baby."

Don't say anything, I told myself, trying not to cry. *Just be a good mother.* Which made me feel worse. Stoli had thrown me completely off balance. I mean, for this to happen, I must have done a bad job. From the moment she was in school, she and her siblings knew the goal was completing college. That was my one firm

line. All five of them would be sent out of the nest with
a degree and hopefully the tools to use it to support
themselves and do some good for others.

But it was complicated. I am not Stoli's birth
mother; we adopted her. How could she not keep this
baby? How could we all not?

As a family, we have always supported each other by
loving *and* liking each other. A piece of obituary wisdom came to mind. A wise and newly widowed woman
once told me that the key to her family's affection for
one another was simple: When they were angry they
treated each other as politely as they would company.
She was from Texas originally and had southern man-
ners and grace.

"Do you ever notice," she had asked me when we
were working on her husband's obituary, "how we often
say the most awful things to the people we are closest to?
To prevent regrets in a marriage, with your children or
in-laws, always say please and thank you and keep the
thoughts you wouldn't voice to company to yourself." I

realized if Stoli weren't my child, I would know exactly how to support her. Funny how that works.

I painted the baby's room the color Stoli chose, even though it seemed way too bright to sleep in. I cooked dinners with her, and Chip and I made sure her boyfriend joined us and that we didn't harp at them about future plans. I encouraged pregnant yoga and long walks and prenatal care. When Stoli called from the deli where she worked to say she was queasy and needed crackers, I rushed right over with some and didn't even mention the whole shelfful of crackers right there, where I'd originally bought the ones I had just given her.

It was more than a little unsettling when everyone—family and friends alike—praised how well I was handling the situation.

As if they hadn't expected it?

WHEN THE ULTRASOUND technician made his bimonthly clinic visit, Stoli and Nels invited me to come along. We all stared silently at what looked like a satellite image of a hurricane on the screen.

"I'm pretty sure it's a girl," the technician said.

Stoli will dance this mother-daughter waltz, too.

The technician used a curser to point out knees and a nose in the swirling waters of life's beginnings. He stopped at something contracting and expanding. "Here's her heart. Look at that. It's beautiful," he said.

How can something so tiny hold so much? While you can't see this on an ultrasound image, the capacity for love in a human heart is not limited by its size. The invisible part of a mother's heart is the strongest and most flexible because it enlarges with each child and grandchild. Rather than divide the heart's chambers into smaller rooms as the family grows, love multiplies them.

In a maternity ward delivery room six months later, at two in the morning, Stoli was ready to push. I was so relieved that I burst into a big smile. Nels pressed Stoli's back, I held her hand, and she groaned, straining with her whole body, and thankfully a very responsive baby slid out. A startled, bluish little doll of an infant, all smeared with the white grease of the womb and reaching her brand-new hands and feet up into the air for the very first time. As she was placed on Stoli's breast, my daughter became tearfully wide-eyed. Nels beamed.

The doctor attended to Stoli and the nurses carried little Lani, who, by the second, grew more accustomed to her new environment—all this oxygen and light and her crazy grandmother laughing and crying—to the heat table where I was told to rub her brand-new feet, which were smaller than my old thumbs. Her skin flushed pink, from her miniature ankles to the

The capacity for love in a human heart is not limited by its size. Rather than divide the heart's chambers into smaller rooms as the family grows, love multiplies them.

scalp beneath her wet black hair. I wiped my eyes and willed them to focus. I needed to keep watch so lovely Lani wouldn't accidentally be switched with another newborn. Who wouldn't prefer her to any baby in the hospital? Just look at her.

Stoli was not worried about that at all. My youngest daughter lives in the moment, just the way I say I should but rarely do. Stoli's pregnancy was as relatively easy for her as the birth. As you know, it was a tad more challenging for me. Maybe that's always the case for the mother of the mother-to-be. Why do I only now recall the look on my mother's face when I told her on a trip back east that I was pregnant for the first time at twenty-two? Chip and I hadn't yet celebrated our first anniversary and lived in an unplumbed shack in Anchorage, thousands of miles from my family's New York home.

Today, I hear myself telling Stoli what my mother told me then: "Sleep when the baby is sleeping." If I didn't, my mother warned me, I could get mastitis.

Stoli looked up. "Mastitis?"

"It's an infection in your milk ducts that is very serious."

"Mom, I'll be fine."

I started to remind her not to let anyone near the baby who hasn't sanitized his or her hands, but the peaceful, capable look on my daughter's face while she nursed her daughter stopped me. Instead, I wished Chip were here so he could say, "I told you so," and I could say thank you.

The afternoon of Lani's first day, Nels's aunt arrived, scrubbing her arms to the elbows (and endearing herself to me forever) before reaching for Lani. I was still groggy from attending the early-morning birth and thought at first I was dreaming as Auntie Tanya sailed into the room. To me, she declared I must be Stoli's sister; I was too young to be a grandmother. (Honestly? I did not look my best.) To Stoli, who was puffy-eyed and tired to her marrow, she exclaimed that never had her niece-in-law been so lovely. It was impossible, Auntie Tanya said, that she had just given birth—"Impossible!" To her nephew she said, "Oh Nels, Oh

Nels, Oh Nels! How lucky we are!" Then lightly, reverently, she pressed that newborn's heart to her heart and held on tight as they two-stepped across the linoleum.

I wished I could be like that. So gentle and calm and saying all the right things so sincerely that she made everyone in the room feel special. Watching Tanya, I decided this is the type of grandmother I will strive to be and, with any luck, become. The kind who speaks with exclamation points. This is what the name our first grandchild Caroline gave me—Mimi—is for! It's what Lani will call me now, too, and each grandchild who follows her. By the time I am eighty, I could be Mimi all the time to everyone. A whole new person.

Mimi knows that it's a mother's job to draw the lines but it's a grandmother's job to remind everyone in the family that sometimes you have to move them, and, more important, what the cost of holding those lines might be.

I was worried about all the wrong things when I learned Stoli was pregnant. All I could see were the negatives. Caroline's first word was *yes* and I'm going to do my part to make sure baby Lani's is, too. Yes, my little darling, you are beautiful and brilliant! Yes, the world is wonderful! Yes, yes, and triple yes! There is nothing to worry about because it is almost summertime and your daddy is kind and your mama knows just what you need, and your grandma Mimi is right here, and always will be, with her arms wide open, just on the other side of the garden.

Wear a Personal
Flotation Device

When fisherman Richard Boyce first arrived in Alaska he was tenting on the side of a road and was told to leave: There was no camping allowed. He was stunned. He thought that of all places in the world Alaska should welcome campers. Today, the sandwich board across from his driveway reads: FREE CAMPING. RATES DOUBLE IN JUNE. SENIOR DISCOUNTS AVAILABLE.

Chip and I often saw Richard on our morning bike ride as he was driving to town for coffee. The last time we saw Richard, he pulled his pickup alongside us and even announced our speed, "Twenty miles per hour, twenty-two, back to nineteen," before waving with a smile from behind his red beard, touching the bill of his cap, and calling out, "Have a good day," as he zoomed off.

Richard slipped on his salmon gillnetter and fell overboard at about five in the morning on the Fourth of July. The youngest of his three grown-but-still-young daughters—all just a few years out of college—tossed him a life ring and radioed for help. Fellow fishermen pulled their nets and came to the Boyces' aid. Many arrived in minutes, but Richard wore heavy rain gear and boots, and a strong tidal current pulled him away from the boat and under the water too fast. His body was never recovered. Richard, who had gone to MIT, built that boat, the thirty-nine-foot *Eleanor S.,* named for his oldest daughter, at his cabin on the ridge above his little "campground."

The day Richard died I was helping out at the hot dog table at the Haines July Fourth picnic. I learned that my neighbor J.R. had handed his helm over to a deckhand and then climbed on board the *Eleanor S.* with Richard's daughter for the six-hour trip home. The next woman who reached for a paper plate and bun told me that she felt better knowing J.R. was there. Everyone did. She named a half-dozen fishermen who also turned their boats back and left the lucrative fishing grounds to escort the *Eleanor S.* home. Once the flotilla was spotted near Battery Point, many in the holiday crowd walked across the park to the harbor and, from behind the bulkhead railing, silently watched as the tall red-haired girl steered that graceful boat into the slip, hopped off, and tied the dock lines, just the way her father had taught her, and then fell into the arms of her mother.

The next day the front deck of the *Eleanor S.* grew a garden. Jars of flowers wild and cultivated, beribboned bouquets, and handmade wreaths were delivered by people compelled by sorrow to make the boat more beautiful. It felt good to leave my jar of daisies with all the others. A few of Richard's friends were determined to use the momentum of community sorrow and good-will to do something more lasting—to raise money to buy new, state-of-the-art flotation devices in the form of inflatable suspenders for the rain pants of every fisherman in Haines's fleet, about 176 skippers and deckhands.

Richard hadn't been wearing a life jacket. Most fishermen don't. Even the ones who can't swim (more than you'd think) are not fans of the bulky vests that hamper movement. Plus, nets can grab and hold the buckles and fasteners, potentially dragging the wearer to his or her death. Some even believe they are bad luck.

The inflatable suspenders are flat and will replace the elastic straps on the rubber overalls that the deckhands and skippers already wear. Randa Szymanski, whose husband is a fisherman, spearheaded the project. She did the research and then double-checked with her husband and other fishermen to be sure she had found the best type of potential life preserver. They said she had.

My neighbor Will has already picked up his. "Want

to see them?" he asked as I walked by the other day. On his way to the garage he glanced at two of the reasons he'll wear them: his young daughters playing on a swing set. Tricycles and toys were all mixed up in the yard with fishing nets. Better still, while I waited, Will's grandfather-in-law, living proof that fishermen make old bones, said he thought they would work, too, and he was planning on using them. Will returned, smiling, with the blue-and-red suspenders draped over his shoulders. The embroidery on the strap read IN MEMORY OF RICHARD BOYCE.

ⲗⲗⲗ

I HOPE ALL THE fisherman will wear their new suspenders every time they are on the water and no one will ever be lost at sea ever again.

Which is completely wishful thinking.

I asked one young captain who is so very dear to me if he would be wearing the suspenders. When he deadpanned "no," I thought he was joking.

Then he said the suspenders were for "old men,"

that he's a strong swimmer, and he knows what he's doing out there. He declared he wasn't going to hassle with any so-called inflatable suspenders.

I wanted to grab him by his shirt and scream that I'd kill him if he drowned without a life jacket or the suspenders, and I definitely would not write his obituary. Didn't he know that's why we raised twenty thousand dollars, in a place without much money, because we love him, and men and women like him, and want to keep them safe? So for God's sake, and ours—please accept our gift and wear them!

A life jacket might not have saved him. Nothing is guaranteed to keep anyone from dying.

But I didn't say or do any of that.

Yelling at that fearless young captain for not accepting the potentially lifesaving and, at the very least, cautionary message–bearing suspenders won't change his mind. And he was right when he said a life jacket might not have saved Richard. Nothing is guaranteed to keep anyone from dying.

Still, something important has happened as the result of the sudden and tragic death. I know that each time another fisherman, like Will, who actually buckles on those suspenders, even looks at them hanging on the hook in the wheelhouse, he will be reminded both of one good colleague and father and of how much the good people in this town care that he and all the others return to our safe harbor.

So instead of parting in anger, I kissed that captain on the cheek and told him to please, please be careful out there, and that I loved him very much, and that I loved his deckhand even more, since he's my only son.

This much I know for sure: Hope floats.

Be Sure Your Dog Walks You

I bet you didn't know that Emily, she who famously wore white and supposedly never left the house, had a Newfoundland named Carlo who slept in her bedroom (and surely needed to be walked) and lived to be seventeen years old—the same seventeen years that Dickinson produced many of her most enduring poems. Her father gave her the puppy because he was concerned that she didn't get out much. He knew that Carlo would be his daughter's connection to the neighbors. I didn't realize that a new dog would do the same for me.

Our good old dog Forte, a large black flat-coated retriever whom we adopted at age four, came of age in a busy household with five children. His activity revolved around the family. So did mine. When he died at ten, just a few months before our youngest child was out of the house, I missed that loopy dog way more than I should have. I mean, he stole butter right off a table set for the holidays, ate cakes intended for bake sales, was almost always wet thanks to the beach outside our back door, and he slept on the couch.

He also loved me unconditionally. I could almost see the images of my years as a mother of teenagers reflected in his eyes.

Yes, it made perfect sense to say to Chip, "We probably shouldn't get another dog." He agreed and said that now we could travel. People do that when the kids leave home. A dog would tie us down.

But I like it here. I get homesick on the almost five-hour ferry trip to Juneau. I was so used to taking care of everyone—children and dogs—that Forte's loss hit me hard. I was grumpy and teary. Chip and I get along great, but he's a self-sufficient adult. He doesn't need me to care for him the way children and pets had. When I cried while attempting to wash Forte's bowl and put it in storage, he looked over his reading glasses and said, "Why don't we just get a puppy?"

Forte had not endeared Chip to rescued dogs. We both agreed it would be easier to live with a dog whose bad habits were at least of our making. There were no puppies at the Humane Society in Haines or Juneau. A ten-week-old, nearly white golden retriever I named Pearl arrived about a month later on a plane from Anchorage, with several pages of operating instructions taped to her kennel. For starters, she must be walked twice a day. Forte walked himself or took off with whoever passed by. Did I mention this was January?

With no children at home to tire her out, it was up to me. Out the door to the beach we went, with Pearl barking hello at the waves and wind. I saw a woman up ahead who was reading a book while walking two golden retrievers, one very old and one younger. We'd met before (this is a small place) but did not know each other well. Of course she melted at the sight of Pearl's stubby puppy tail and scooped her up and inhaled her puppy-breath scent.

"Why don't you join us?" she asked.

"Sure."

Our talk was all dogs, and I learned so much from my canine-wise companion, who'd studied naturopathy and acupuncture for animals, had no children, and adored her golden retrievers—and the beach marches with them in all weather.

The next day, Sabine brought Pearl a container of her homemade dog food, and we met her friend Beth. She, too, had recently buried an old dog but was caring for her in-laws' Lab while they were out of town for a few weeks, so we all proceeded together, tossing balls and sticks for the dogs and becoming better acquainted. Beth and I knew each other from hospice meetings— she is the administrator and I'm a board member—but did not hang out socially. She's busy, too.

Turns out Beth and Sabine had a daily date to walk the beach and invited Pearl and me to join them at seven the next morning, before they went to work.

"In the dark?"

"Headlamps," they said in unison.

I thought, if I don't wake up and step out the door when I see those lights bobbing in the snowy dark, and answer their waves with a "Wait for me!" now, when will I?

That was about two years ago.

⁓

BETH HADN'T PLANNED on getting another dog, either, but I think Pearl and I inspired her. (Of course little Lucy is a golden retriever.) I know my bond with Pearl is in many ways tighter than was my bond with Forte, and it's because of the routine we both hate to miss. Some days it takes a lot longer to cover the three miles of shoreline; my friends and I have so much to say about all kinds of things that it slows us down. And sometimes we are reluctant to end the conversation at the parking area, so we take another lap, much to the dogs' delight.

One morning we were talking about friendship and Beth said her mother taught her that if she wanted to have good friends all she had to do was be one. I haven't done that as well as I could have. I don't have a lot of close friends. My free time revolved around my family or community events and boards like hospice and the Haines Library, on which I've served for years. My other activities were all with Chip—running and cycling mostly—and time was tight when there were seven of us for dinner every night and I was the cook.

But that was then. Things change. I can, too. It's not too late.

~ల్లి~

WHEN I SAW A BOOK of dog poems at the store, I ordered three copies, one for each of us. After the new soil in my garden proved weak, Beth arrived with four thriving zucchini plants, each in its own washtub planter. "I have way too many, anyway," she said. On another evening Sabine stopped by with a tin of her spicy homemade cocoa mix.

Just about daily, we take turns listening to and sharing all kinds of private, personal, women-friend

················•ᴠ•················

We aren't walking the dogs, anymore.
These are people walks, with dogs.

················•ᴀ•················

things—or at least what I have always imagined would be women-friend talk—from what to say to a relative on her deathbed to how we feel about God or which one we could live without more easily, wine or coffee? We discuss local and national issues, too, from health-care to school funding. Bouncy Pearl provokes an oc-casional growl from Sabine's gray-muzzled old gal. The last time that happened I realized that we three are now good enough friends to also have a rare snappy mo-ment, too, and that we forget them as quickly as our pets do. Some mornings we fret about climate change. Others, we silently observe a great blue heron fishing in the shallows, grateful that the dogs have run up ahead and won't scare it off. All of our conversations are safe under what we call "the dome of silence," as in, "what happens on a dog walk stays on a dog walk." Well, except we aren't walking the dogs, anymore. These are people walks, with dogs.

The other morning we reached the end of our walk but continued to visit. Beth would be gone on vacation for the next month. She was worried about leaving her new dog with her stepdaughter, who works full time and has two young children. Walking the dog will be too much for her. "We'll take care of Lucy," Sabine and I said at the same time.

That's what friends are for.

Maybe Chip and I will take a trip, too, now that the kids are grown and I have friends who will watch Pearl.

That's what happens when you get a dog.

Send a
Forwarding Address

When I volunteered to help clean out Russ's cabin before it was auctioned off to benefit Hospice of Haines, I thought I'd be there for an hour, not all afternoon. I did not envision sitting outside in the spring sun for hours sorting his bills, receipts, and especially all those cards for recycling—whites, colors, cardboard.

Russ had willed his home and its contents, including his TV, easy chair, and a shelfful of military-themed videotapes, to our volunteer hospice organization, which had arranged for his care after a lifetime of smoking caught up with him. When hospice board president Nancy Schnabel suggested that fellow board members Bud Barber and I clean up the place before the sale, we were happy to help. Compared to other hospice work, this was easy on the heart. Besides, it wouldn't take long. Russ's cabin only had two small rooms.

He lived a simple life but was not a woodsy hermit. The place is on a main road at the edge of town. A few curious drivers slowed to check out Bud and me; Susie, pushing Patience in a stroller, walked by twice before inquiring about our activity. After that, Bud laughed. "Wow, we sure are giving people something to talk about—'Bud and Heather are moving into Russ's old place.'"

There's not a lot of privacy in a small town.

I was determined to protect Russ's. So when I opened the first cigar box filled with greeting cards, I tossed them without a peek. By the tenth box, though,

I looked more closely at each envelope. Who were they all from? Why had he saved them? What did they say?

Not much beyond the publisher's sentimental verse followed by a handwritten "Thinking of you," or "Hope you are well," or on one tucked into an envelope postmarked in Maine, "So glad to finally meet you Uncle Russ."

While researching his obituary, I had called his brother back east and learned that Russ had been born and reared in Maine, joined the Army right out of high school, and then disappeared by degrees. Pretty soon, there was no forwarding address. No phone calls, no letters, no cards. Nothing. Russ didn't contact his family for thirty-eight years. *Thirty-eight years.* It was like a Marilynne Robinson novel.

I asked why. What had happened? His brother told me Russ had spent that time riding the rails. He had been a real-life hobo before a searching family member discovered him alive and well in Alaska. I had hoped to learn why he had been gone all those years; that must be the crux of Russ's life story, I thought. But his brother didn't share the reason, if he even knew, and instead said all that mattered was that Russ had been found and that, by the time he died, the family had been happily reunited for several years. Relatives had visited Russ in Haines, and he had traveled to Maine. The brothers played music together. The nephews enjoyed fishing in Alaska.

I BELIEVE GRATITUDE comes from a place in your soul that knows the story could have ended differently, and often does, and I also know that gratitude is at the heart of finding the good in this world—especially in our relationships with the ones we love. I see proof of this all the time.

When I was writing Pete Lapham's obituary, his wife, Diana, told me that when they learned Pete's cancer wasn't curable, he chose to stop treatments and come home from the hospital before he was too sick to appreciate his final days. It was a gift, she said, that she and his sons and their friends had that time together. She didn't say she wished she'd never had to open this particular surprise package, though it had to be true.

Unlike Russ, Pete's whereabouts was never in doubt. He never left his hometown, so his family (and everyone else in the community, for that matter) always knew where to find him. Pete was so responsible that after his first marriage ended and his ex-wife moved away, her father continued to live with Pete. And every day for more than thirty years, in rain, sun, or snow, Pete patrolled roads as the state Department of Transportation foreman. With a smile and a wave, he greeted friends and strangers alike from behind the windshield of the plow truck or grader.

Russ, on the other hand, didn't smile much. His favorite job was mowing the cemetery. In a way, Russ's people were my people: We both befriended the dead. When I turned in his obituary, my editor, Tom, and I argued over its length. I thought the "Amazing Grace" prodigal son story was worth sharing. That old hymn

*I believe gratitude comes from
a place in your soul that knows the story
could have ended differently, and often does,
and I also know that gratitude is at the heart
of finding the good in this world.*

about being lost and then found, sung at so many graves, finally made sense to me after hearing the way Russ's family welcomed him back after all those years of uncertainty.

Maybe because I am a mother, my heart inclined more toward Russ than Tom's did. My only son tends to ramble more than my daughters do, and while I understood that it is possible to lose touch gradually, when I learned how seamlessly that could become nearly permanent, it terrified me. I wanted to include Russ's history as a warning, so that future sons and their families would fill out the change-of-address forms and send cards, or at least texts, as they roamed far from home.

Last year, the only physical address I had for my son, Christian, was at his friend's house in the tiny ski resort where he spent some of his winter. Sure I had his cell number, but when he hadn't replied to my calls for eight days, I was only half joking when I texted, "Should I call the state troopers and report a missing person?"

The photo of my handsome, long-haired, six-foot-three, twenty-four-year-old only son that I keep at my desk is his kindergarten school portrait. That eager-to-please, smiling little boy with the clip-on tie and slicked-back cowlick lives inside a quiet, adventurous, commercial fisherman now, but they both have the same eyes that I have loved since he opened them in the delivery room.

∼⟋⟍∼

RUSS'S MOTHER DIED before the family found him, but on her deathbed she made her other children promise that when Russ turned up (and she knew he would) they'd give him her Bible. In it was a note. "Wherever you are I hope you are happy and well," she wrote in shaky old-fashioned cursive. That detail did not make the edited obituary. Neither did her formal inscription in the Bible bound for Russ: "Remember me always as I have always you since the day you left us."

After Russ's brother delivered the Bible, his relatives must have begun writing to his Alaska address, mailing him all these Christmas, birthday, and even Thanksgiving cards, and he, in turn, must have been so grateful that he saved what appeared to be every single one. Did he know someone else would have to sort and toss them?

Sitting in the shade of Russ's cabin that day, bagging so many cards with turkeys and cornucopia pictures on them for Bud to take to the recycling center, I thought about how it had never occurred to me to send a Thanksgiving card. Other holidays, yes, but Thanksgiving? No doubt they said a blessing for Russ at the family Thanksgiving table all those years he was missing, and I bet they acknowledged their gratitude when he came back. If you think about it, isn't that why we send every card and letter? Because we are grateful for the relationship with the recipient?

⁓

RUSS DIED QUIETLY AND was buried in the cemetery he had tended, following a small graveside service. When Pete died, the volunteer fire department, of which Pete was a lifetime member, drove the flashing fleet of red trucks to his house, where they lined up in two solemn rows while more firemen carried Pete's body out through the aisle. The memorial service was held in the arts center theater, because the church couldn't seat the four hundred or so mourners.

Diana asked me to deliver Pete's eulogy. I spoke about the way he lived, remembering the spring in his walk and how he made that effortless one-armed leap up into the cab of a big old plow truck or idling front-end loader. I knew the feeling the sight of him gave his friends and family. It was the same way I feel when I see my son walking up the porch steps each summer when he returns home. I'm sorry that Russ's mother did not live to have that joy.

After the funeral, Diana sent me a pretty thank-you card with a brief personal note at the bottom. It was nothing special; it could have been in the recycle bin with Russ's, but I cried when I read it like I hadn't at Pete's service. My contribution mattered. I had done something good for someone else. I tucked the card in my desk's miscellany drawer. I see it every time I search for a stamp. Sometimes I hold it and open it and remember Pete. Mostly, it reminds me to send cards. An e-mail is not the same at all. You never know when a card mailed today will be received, but someone will read it, sooner or later, and be thankful.

I'm so glad I volunteered to clean an old man's cabin, and that he saved all those cards sent by all those people who loved him in spite of his absence. Otherwise, I might not have made sure I reached my son to tell him how much I love him. And, more important, that he needs to be sure we have his address before he leaves this fall. I'm already composing a Thanksgiving card.

Hop 'til You Drop

After I was hit by a truck while riding my bike, I had to learn to walk again, and before I could even imagine running or cycling again, I had to regain my strength. A broken pelvis had immobilized me for months. It was hard, really hard, both physically and emotionally. When you used to be an athlete, it's embarrassing and humbling not to be able to complete the simplest balance drills or to be sore and tired after a half-hour stroll. I put on a brave face, but a lot of times that year I felt like the boxer Marlon Brando portrayed in *On the Waterfront,* who moaned, "I coulda been a contender." Every sentence in my head began with *I used to . . .*

The story of my accident and recovery might make an okay movie, but I knew all the sweat and hard work in the world wouldn't help me run another marathon. Not with my compromised bones and frayed sinews. Other competitive sports were out for a while, too. Dr. Marnie Hartman, our town's only physical therapist, and a great one, suggested a new "sport": Morning Muscles, her women's exercise class. It wasn't exactly the same as training for a triathlon, or even a hike up nearby Mount Riley, but I had to begin somewhere, and I am a good patient. When a doctor tells me to do something, I listen.

Now, I make sure I'm awake every Tuesday and Thursday at 5:15 a.m. so I can be at the class by 6:00. On the day of our last class, it had snowed, again, so I tugged my coat over my pajamas and waded through the driveway to see if I could make it out in four-wheel drive.

When I came back inside, Chip, who is always up before I am, joked that I could just shovel the driveway instead. Thanks to three years of Morning Muscles, I could, if I wanted to. I am so much stronger and more flexible. I even raced my bicycle again last summer. But I'm still braving the dark and the weather to make it to class, because there's way more to it than the sit-ups.

Everyone begins Mornings Muscles for different reasons, but I suspect all have to do with being less than thrilled with our bodies. We are all women between about thirty-five and sixty-five, so you can guess what's on our minds: Michelle Obama's arms, looking better at the beach, muscle and bone loss, six-pack abs. Youth, beauty, truth. Does my butt look big?

But something happens over the weeks, months, and years of regular workouts. Pretty soon it's not about the tummy roll or the wobbly thighs or even how many crunches we can now complete in a minute. That's all beside the point. It's about doing the best with what we've got and appreciating our scarred-up, well-used, stretch-marked, marvelously individual bodies just as they are—"without judgment," as Marnie says—even as we strive to improve what they can do, one lunge and squat at a time, before collapsing in sweaty heaps on the floor. (It's very good that there isn't a video on YouTube.)

I'm feeling pretty good about myself now that I can finally hold that plank for sixty seconds. Better

The secret to aging more cheerfully is to play like a child.

than I have in years, actually. This is what Dr. George Sheehan, who wrote one of my favorite books about running, meant by "Sweat cleanses from the inside. It comes from places a shower will never reach."

Also, there is no *I used to . . .* in the Morning Muscles routine; since I didn't do this before the accident, I'm still riding the upward curve and, while I know that nothing guarantees a longer life, keeping fit makes mine richer.

I should have begun this kind of exercise years ago, when I was running so much, because it would have helped me run better and no doubt prevented some of my minor injuries. I wish I'd learned a lesson from writing Harriet Stoll's obituary. I did note that the very proper little old lady's neighbor revealed that Harriet had spent hours a day jumping on a trampoline. I thought it was funny, even nutty. Now I know better. The secret to aging more cheerfully is to play like a child.

If you could see us rolling on and off our exercise balls in Morning Muscles it would make you feel just about as good as it does us. I wonder what Harriet was thinking about as she bounced and twisted, especially at her advanced age. Maybe she wasn't thinking at all but just having a grand old time. Like her, I, too, break into a sweat just about every day, because I still can, and because, for me, the effort equals the reward.

I've never regretted a workout. That's the time when

I am that kid on the playground again, swinging with all my strength, hand over hand across the monkey bars. Sure it's hard, but when I'm done I'm as proud of myself as that ten-year-old me was when she shouted, "Mom, look what I can do!"

Hold on Tight

There's no easy way to say this," a former neighbor who had moved to Juneau years ago said when we bumped into each other recently and had finished giving updates on our families and activities, "so I might as well blurt it out. Will you write my obituary?"

"You look so healthy," I said.

"My expiration date was three months ago," she said. What can a person say in response to that, except, yes, I'll do whatever you ask of me?

A few days later I received an e-mail reminding me to keep her breast cancer diagnosis confidential. She had attached the outline of her bio and concluded with additional instructions: "I don't want you to list the people who survive me. I don't like that term and I don't like to limit them; there are so many more than my immediate family. I also don't want you to write 'lost her battle with cancer' or 'after a long struggle with cancer.' I live with cancer. It is what it is. It is my life, not some kind of war with myself. And please don't say that I never complained. I hate that—what's with that? I complain all the time. Cancer is so UNFAIR."

I was immediately reminded of a favorite expression of my father's. Every opportunity he gets, and there are many more, it seems, as he ages, my father will say, "Life's not fair." Then he'll shrug and add, "So?" Usually he's speaking of small injustices. His favorite team played better but the other team got lucky and won. The tomatoes were the best he'd ever grown, until the windstorm ripped them off the vines.

But Rene's situation is *really* unfair.

Sometimes I wish I were a sports columnist instead of an obituary writer. They get to write about fun and games. In another life I might have been. Who knows. My father used to call me the Mickey Mantle of Ruth Place, the street on which I grew up. When I was ten years old, my dad ran into the house from the commuter train station a few blocks away and hugged all three of his daughters, but especially me, the only baseball player. He had heard that a little girl, about my age, had been struck and killed by a delivery truck while riding her bicycle to the nearby ball fields. All he knew then was that there was a bloody baseball mitt in the road. We learned later that night that it belonged to my neighborhood friend.

A few weeks after little Marie's funeral, my father and I played catch in the backyard. "Two hands, keep your eye on the ball," he coached as we tossed high flies over the clothesline. It's advice I still try to follow. Even a grown woman could do worse than keep her eye on what is important in life and hold onto it tight with both hands. That day, I asked my father why a stupid truck had killed my friend. That's the first time I recall hearing him say, "Life's not fair. So?" He didn't say it with any bitterness. He said it without breaking the rhythm of the toss and catch or altering the tone of his voice. Life is unfair. The ball soars up in the air and

*Even a grown woman could do worse
than keep her eye on what is important in life
and hold onto it tight with both hands.*

comes down. Sometimes you make the play, sometimes you don't. So? You pay more attention next time, and keep your head in the game until the last out.

Rene and I corresponded by e-mail and text message frequently, and soon we were, if not exactly friends, at least pen pals with an oddly intimate connection. When I e-mailed her that I'd be coming to Juneau to visit my oldest daughter, she invited me over for tea so we could prioritize the details she had already sent me and come up with the core of her obituary—names, dates, events of note—everything that would help me make sure her life was documented accurately. I had never before had the chance to ask one of my subjects about what was important in his or her life, what was worth writing down, and I was curious and apprehensive. When Eliza dropped me off, I guessed the visit would take about an hour and told her that I'd call for a ride when we were through.

Rene poured tea from a handmade clay pot and we settled into the window seat her husband had built in their cozy living room and fell right to the task. When we had covered all the basics and reached the part of my job where I usually leave a mourning household with a list of friends they've given me to contact for a fond memory, Rene answered a question I hadn't asked but wanted to know so badly: How does her impending death change the way she will spend her remaining months? Will she go to Europe? Take up skydiving? Volunteer in an orphanage? Plant a garden? Write a book?

"What is it I really want to do?" she said. "I want an ordinary life with my family, and to teach school."

She loves spending her days with first graders, she told me, because little children live in the present and she values that now more than ever. "Each child comes to me with a set of needs and I have to meet them where they're at. I don't have time to worry about my own problems." Rene was so calm, so sure, and so steady. Mostly though, she wasn't afraid. She even smiled after making a joke about "playing the cancer card" some days in order to skip the housework.

I'm the one who cannot understand why this is happening. I'm the one who is angry and sad. This is so unfair. I am not good at feeling uncomfortably emotional. My heart banged against my ribs. My hands shook. I didn't want to upset her. I wanted to help, so I concentrated on my notebook, pretending I was checking facts. The page was all scribbles that I hoped I'd be able to read when I needed these names and dates later to flesh out the obituary of Rene's brief and happy life.

I know a good story when I hear one and I can recognize a sad ending even when it's looking me in the eye and laughing. This one was about Rene's courage and her grace. She was telling me hers for a reason. She knew then, the way I do now, that it is important to share.

That's why, at that moment, even though I was sure I was about to crumble and even though I knew, just knew, this was more than I was capable of dealing with, I chose to be the person she believed I was. I pretended I was up to the job she had given me. I promised her I would write a fine obituary.

Rene yawned. I'd been at her house for three hours. I had forgotten she was terminal and that this must have been exhausting. I said I'd call Eliza, but she insisted on driving me back to my daughter's house. In the car, she said she'd like to stay in touch because talking like this about death didn't shock me the way it does others. "You understand."

I was embarrassed by her frankness and wanted to correct her, to say, no, you're wrong, I don't get it at all, but I said, "Thank you, I think." Then I said something I normally would be too shy to articulate—but after our visit I knew I must. There may not be another opportunity. I came right out and told Rene that I really liked and admired her. She said she felt the same way about me.

She drove and we kept talking, like girlfriends now. She didn't want to burden her family and she couldn't speak the way she could with me to her dearest old friends and coworkers—she didn't want to depress them or have them feel sorry for her. "I made the decision that I don't really want people to know, but sometimes someone will complain about something in a school e-mail and I'm like, really?" She worried that not sharing the gravity of her illness was selfish. "I don't want my friends to feel betrayed," she said. "What do you think?"

"If you can't do what you want when you are dying of cancer, when can you?" I replied. I did suggest that she might want to let a few more friends in on the situation, because it would be good to have support and I was sure they'd want to be there for her. Like me, they'd find her honesty inspiring.

Suddenly a bright light blinded us.

It was not God.

It was a car coming our way. The driver was passing in a double-yellow-line zone. Rene swerved, tires grinding on the rough shoulder, before muscling her station wagon back onto the road.

She whispered, "That was close."

I exhaled. "You know, you may not die of cancer."

She laughed and gripped the steering wheel with both hands and held on for every moment left in her dear life.

My father was right about keeping your eyes on the ball and holding on tight with two hands. I could almost see him then, shrugging somewhere in the darkness and I definitely heard him say, "Life's not fair. So?"

I hugged Rene good-bye and stepped into Eliza's hallway. I kicked off my boots and hung up my coat and then sat with the dog's red head in my lap, on Eliza's new/used Craigslist couch. I accepted yet another cup of tea and listened intently while my oldest daughter talked about her struggles with a few challenging students (she teaches fourth grade), the success of her coed ice hockey team, the new friends she has made while walking her dog, her boyfriend's carpentry skills, and all about her ordinary, busy, normal—and I'm sure Rene would agree—wonderful life.

Put on a Costume
Now and Then

You'd think as a mother of five I would have gotten the hang of creating costumes for Halloween. I never did, but I have learned that there are benefits to wearing one, both for your own sake and to make someone else happy.

I was trick-or-treating with my children one stormy year—I used giant silver trash bags to dress them as raindrops, for which they have never forgiven me—when a neighbor complimented me on my Halloween costume.

I wasn't wearing one. I had pulled on my rubber rain gear—bibs and jacket, fishing boots and waterproof hat. (It was pouring and we were on foot.) The hat was a yellow sou'wester—the kind you see on old salts who are advertising clam chowder—which may have been part of the misunderstanding. I laughed and thanked her, but the comment stuck with me because it could have been true. When I bought that hat I might have chosen the dark green model to blend in more with the weather, but I grabbed the yellow one because it was brighter, and I knew wearing something so bold would make walking through town in the rain more fun.

All the world really is a stage, and men and women alike dress for parts every day. When I interview a family for an obituary I always dress up a little more than usual, out of respect for them, and so they see that I have a different role from the person they know from the softball games or the farmer's market.

The adventure tour guides who work here every summer buy the canvas carpenter pants and brown rubber fishing boots worn by locals as soon as they arrive. Some purchase well-used ones at the Salvation Army thrift store to appear even more in character. Sometimes old-timers make fun of this, but I think it's smart. When the guides look like they belong, they feel like they do, so they take their jobs more seriously. Some of them become so fond of those boots that they move here so they can wear them all year long.

....

I knew wearing something
so bold would make walking through
town in the rain more fun.

....

My mother was a teacher and a principal. She wore jeans and sneakers at home but a skirted suit with heels to school. She taught me the importance of dressing for the occasion, out of respect for others and for yourself. When I served on the school board, I did not wear jeans and rubber boots to important or contentious meetings. I chose what I called my "schoolteacher outfit." For about twenty years I wore the same dark wool dress and clogs whenever I needed a suit of emotional armor.

I miss that dress. My mother-in-law bought it for me at a shop outside of Boston. It was expensive, but she said it was a classic that I'd be able to wear for years. Which is why, when my daughters helped me clean my closet and wanted to toss it, I pleaded, "It's a classic!"

Had I really looked, as they insisted, like a cross between my mother and Florence Henderson from *The Brady Bunch* when I wore it? Oh well. I kind of liked that spunky TV mom with all those children.

Maybe I kept that dress for so long because it was a gift from my mother-in-law and I was hoping some of her style and confidence would rub off on me. So much depends on what to wear.

I agreed to give it to the Salvation Army but now I wish I had saved it, if only to pair with a short frosted wig for the annual Halloween party at the Pioneer Bar. I usually don't go because I'm so costume-challenged. The party is an opportunity to look like the person you sometimes wish you were, for just a little while. Take Allen. He works at Chip's lumberyard, dotes on his widowed mother (he brought her on a cruise last year), and all of his ex-wives' and current girlfriend's children adore him. When the children of a former girlfriend forget their school lunches, they still ask the teacher to call Allen, and he'll bring one. And then there's the three-story cinder-block castle under construction in his backyard. He designed it with Legos. It makes complete sense that one Halloween Allen was Batman. His custom-fitted costume was so real it could have been in the movies. With a mask and cape, he looked every bit the generous do-gooder, which in a very real way, he is. (Although I'm not sure he'll ever finish that Batcave.)

Then there's the mindful vegetarian who cuts her own bangs and plays Haydn on her cello and, while she will remain nameless because she managed to pull off this neat trick and I won't reveal her secret, I will say that she donned a platinum-blonde wig, false eyelashes, lots of makeup, and a specially enhanced Dolly Parton–style dress and totally put one over on everyone. A whisky-drinking regular who is also a big game—hunting guide sat on his stool, ignoring the party and chatting with the bartender, until Dolly Parton sat down next to him and flirted. He was smitten.

The last time I drastically altered my appearance (on purpose) was for my dad's retirement party a few years ago. My youngest sister, Suzanne, who also lives in Haines, and I were invited to the event, held at an uptown Manhattan restaurant. My father was in the designer watch business, so it would be glitzy. Suzanne and I spent anxious hours digging in our closets and shopping online, though we agreed that our best Alaska dress-up shoes would be fine: black Dansko clogs. (Mine are patent leather.) It would be dark and no one would be looking at our shoes.

The first thing our stylish middle sister, Kathleen, an Upper East Sider, did when we arrived was veto the clogs. She called her favorite shop and found two pairs of dress shoes in our sizes and ordered us to pick them up before the party. Then she handed me a lot of bulky jewelry and Suzanne a whole new outfit.

I suspected this was coming, so I didn't get mad about the hundred-twenty-five-dollar ballet flats that hurt my feet and will ultimately become part of my granddaughters' dress-up kit. But Suzanne did. "It doesn't matter what you wear. It is who you are that counts," she said, noting that if we were from "Denmark or someplace," no one would tell us not to wear clogs to a party. "It's so rude." We three adult siblings regressed right back to junior high, and since our mother had passed away and my daughters weren't there, we had no one to mediate.

When will I be grown up enough to have the kind of confidence, or chutzpah, as they say in New York, to tell my middle sister what to wear the way she tells me, or to express my indignation as boldly as my little sister does? (Suzanne nixed the demure flats in favor of red high heels, which she threatened to bill Kathleen for.) Or even just acquire the plain, Kate Hepburn kind of gumption to walk into a room in the clothes I feel most comfortable in, regardless of where it is, or whom I am with, or what people may think.

Not this trip east, anyway.

But no, I do not believe I chickened out when I settled on the best costume for the occasion and made my New York family happy. Clogs are fine for Alaskan "more formal than normal" events, but in Manhattan, a different sort of footgear is sometimes required. Also, if how we dressed for my father's big night was that important to Dad and Kathleen, whose style, grace, and good humor I adore, we two Alaskans could, for an evening, wear the uniform of well-to-do urbane women.

When I told Suzanne to pretend it was Halloween, she snorted, and then relaxed.

Actually, we had fun dressing up like Cinderellas. My father was visibly proud of his three "girls," and we were just as proud of him as we listened to all the toasts and stories from the office where he'd spent more time than he had at home when we were children. Suzanne and I nibbled on caviar toast and sipped champagne, as if we did it more than once a decade or so.

In the cab back to our hotel Suzanne was a new woman. She wondered out loud if Kathleen would let her keep her outfit. Then she looked at her new shoes and laughed. "I just hope this rig doesn't turn into a pumpkin at midnight or I'll have to walk in these things."

Take the Kind of Happiness
That Comes Your Way

Betty had a difficult beginning. She didn't get enough oxygen while she was stuck in the birth canal and it seemed that she might not live. Only the heroic efforts of our babysitter saved her. Betty is a cat.

While Tammy was watching my little girls—at the time Eliza was two and a half, Sarah one and a half—she'd brought along her pregnant cat, Mindy. Tammy's apartment was upstairs from ours. We had no idea Mindy was close to delivering or that such a little calico would have so many kittens, so it was a big surprise when Mindy had seven in the closet of my daughters' bedroom. Betty was the last one out and it was clear that she was not quite right. Tammy massaged her and held her to a teat.

I know kittens are cute, and cats are okay. Some people adore them. I have a good friend who has had up to half a dozen at a time. Which is how I know I'm allergic to them. I am a dog person. So the next day, after the new cat family had stabilized, I told Tammy that she needed to take them home. That night, I heard something at the door. When I opened it, Mindy ran by me with a kitten in her mouth. She relayed each one, by the scruffs of their tiny necks, back to the closet. We repeated this kitty parade three or four more times before I gave up and said that they might as well stay until they were weaned. Eight weeks later, six fat, playful (FREE!) kittens were scooped up within days of placing the ad in the paper.

Skinny, shy Betty was not. Her mother had become more and more hostile toward her, so she couldn't go

back upstairs with Tammy. I had small children who
adored those kittens. Especially the wobbly runt. She

*Her quiet ways kept us vigilant about her
well-being. Isn't it always the ones who don't
ask for your time and attention who receive it
more willingly than those who clamor for it?*

might not live long and that would be a hard lesson
for them.

Poor Betty had issues with balance, intellect, and
even instinct—we had to feed her or she wouldn't eat.
Betty didn't even flinch when our husky, who could
have eaten her, poked a wet snout at her. She also didn't
scratch the girls or try to sit on my lap and make me
sneeze. She was content to purr a few feet away. Betty
was clean and even pretty, as cats go. A classic white-
chested gray tabby. She allowed the girls to wrap her
in a blanket and tuck her into the doll's bed. When

they carried her around the house, she would go limp, draped like a soft horseshoe over their forearms. My mother called her "the cat with no bones."

While Betty didn't thrive, she didn't backslide, either. She grew into an adult cat, but kept that trusting kitten look in her eyes. Her coat remained short and sleek. Maybe that's why her fur didn't bother me. Betty wasn't the kind of pet who demanded or required any attention at all, and yet her quiet ways kept us vigilant about her well-being. Isn't it always the ones who don't ask for your time and attention who receive it more willingly than those who clamor for it? She looked sweet as a stuffed toy when she napped on the sofa, and was as still. If I sat next to her she did not even open her eyes, much less move toward me. I welcomed her raggedy purr as a sign that all was well with the household, and my life.

Betty never became a normal eater. She refused wet cat food, or even fresh salmon leftovers, in favor of dry food her whole life. Chip fed her on the windowsill to keep the dogs out of her bowl. (Betty would never fight for anything.) Every morning Chip would fill Betty's dish, then shake it so she could hear it was full, and she'd jump up and eat. If he set it down without a sound she wouldn't know it was there and would think she must have eaten already. Likewise, if someone hadn't realized she'd been fed and thought she looked hungry and repeated the process, she'd eat again. I had to watch her weight when eager children overfed her.

In those years my own babies kept coming and soon there were four, and then five. I never feared Betty would be one of those bad cats that infant-care books warn about, the ones who leap into cribs. She was not a cat you had to shoo off the counters, either. As the family, and Betty, matured, we spent weekends and much of the summer at a cabin in the woods. She'd sit on a child's lap in the car on the drive out there and then walk up the trail with us, or let someone carry her, more like a lady's lapdog than a cat. She was slower and quieter than the husky, Lab, and corgi that she outlived. At the cabin, by day she'd sit on a stump and watch the wind move the birch leaves, and at night she'd sleep on the foot of a child's bunk. When her dish was rattled she'd jump up and eat.

Observing her, I couldn't help but be amused, even in the middle of a hectic day during the busiest years of my life. You know that game you play with little kids, the one where you point to a make-believe spill on their shirt and then when they look down, you give their chin and nose a little flick? Betty prompted a similar reaction in me about once a month. I'd think she had a smudge on her chin and try to wipe it off, only to realize, again, that it was a birthmark. Her "dirty" face fooled me every time.

I never had to teach my children to be kind to animals or that they require regular meals, fresh air, and shelter. Betty did. I know she was just a cat—a silly, simple, unremarkable critter in so many ways—but she shared our home with us in the momentous years of family rearing and witnessed all our trials and joys: Thanksgivings and sleepovers, from potty training to the prom. Betty was eating on the windowsill on all five of our children's first days of school. I made sure there was always a Valentine card "from Betty" for each of them. Even her name was funny. I have no idea where my kids came up with "Betty."

Mostly, Betty made me feel like I was a good mother because when she was in the yard—or for that matter, the living room—our house, like Crosby, Stills, Nash & Young sang, really was finer, even with just one cat in the yard.

In the long run, the cat I didn't want turned out to be one of the most endearing pets I've ever known. And it was a *very* long run, almost eighteen years. One morning, when our two daughters with whom Betty had begun her life were away at college and three other teenagers were still asleep, Chip went downstairs to fill the woodstove and found Betty cold on the hearthrug.

"Are you sure?" I said, as we looked down at her. "Could we take her to the vet and see?"

He assured me this was an easy end to a gentle life. Betty appeared to be sleeping, and she was in one of her favorite places. Even in death, the good old cat was no trouble at all.

When I began to cry, Chip teared up, which undid me. Then he cradled Betty in a towel and said he'd bury her down on the beach next to the big rock, so we'd still have her in sight.

Betty was proof that Jean Webster was right when she wrote, "The world is full of happiness, and plenty to go round, if you are only willing to take the kind that comes your way."

Which is a roundabout way of saying that, if someone else's cat has kittens in your closet, keep the runt.

Practice
Staggered Breathing

I sing spirituals when I'm weary and, just as they promise, I'm refreshed. Country songs are my choice when I'm hiking. Yodeling keeps the bears away. I have a CD of *Guys and Dolls* that I sing along to when I'm on my way to an interview for an obituary. Hollering, "Sit down, sit down, sit down, sit down, sit down, you're rocking the boat," alone in the car clears my emotional deck so I won't cry as soon as the widow opens her door.

I will never sing a solo except in the privacy of my Subaru. I do not have a great voice. But I can read music and carry a tune and am a solid though definitely not leading member of the choir. I mean that literally: the Haines A Cappella Women's Chorus.

There are two dozen women (give or take a handful) who practice at the museum on Thursday nights from six to seven, under the volunteer direction of Nancy Nash. Gathered together in that space we become something better, sometimes it even feels greater, than the sum of our singing parts. We stand in a circle or sit on folding chairs in the main gallery, learn new songs, and belt out old familiar ones surrounded by yellow-and-black Chilkat Indian blankets and other displays that illustrate our town's history—much of which has been written by, and nearly all of it preserved by, women like us.

Elisabeth Sheldon Hakkinen founded the museum using the objects her father, a grocer, collected. Native Tlingit women wove the distinctive Chilkat dance robes. There's a modern-day Chilkat weaver in our group. Haines is named for Mrs. Francina Haines, a Presbyterian missionary, and there are several pastors' wives who sing with us. Nancy Nash even works in the museum archives part time when she's not giving piano lessons in her living room.

All around us is a lot of colorful, somewhat random stuff—there's a glittering lens from an old lighthouse, two bearskin rugs, a reproduction wood-and-sinew dogsled made for a gold rush–era movie filmed here in the eighties, blue-and-white antique china, some old dolls that were Elisabeth's when she was a child, and elaborately beaded sealskin slippers, too. All proof of how individual community members may add a bit of sparkle to one area or another, but collectively our pooled talents and interests create, as my daughters say, an impressive pile of bling. You don't have to sing in a choir to see that a group of committed people who care about something that makes life a little brighter, and work hard at it, can accomplish more together than alone, but it helps.

THE CHOIR DOESN'T SO much rehearse as learn songs and then sing for the fun of it. We don't appear in public all that often, but when we are asked to perform at special events, like the fiftieth anniversary of the ferry system, the Women's Club convention, or a funeral, we are prepared. As much as I love to sing, especially tucked securely into the alto section, I feared I could barely make any sound at all the afternoon we found our places on the stage at the memorial service of a good friend who died a young sixty-one from a relatively rare blood disease. No matter how many obituaries I write, I will never get used to talking to someone one day and learning that they've left town, and the entire planet, the next. It may not shock me the way it does others, but that doesn't make it any easier. There is no good in missing someone so badly you can't even hum.

We opened the memorial service with "Dona Nobis Pacem," or "Grant Us Peace." The miracle was that peace not only settled like a shawl on the shoulders of our choir, but it draped the entire hall. By the time we finished our set with "Hope," an Emily Dickinson poem set to an old Irish hymn, our voices had swelled into a river of comfort flowing over all those sad people. They had mostly stopped crying and had settled more comfortably into their seats.

We begin each practice with the same song we sang at the memorial service and this Thursday was no exception. Nancy said she had an idea that would make it sound even better the next time we performed it. She had altered the timing. This was not met with odes to joy. I was not the only one who preferred the round the old way. Our first attempt at the different arrangement sounded okay, but it was difficult to sing without gasping for air. Nancy was not discouraged.

"This is a perfect opportunity to practice staggered breathing," was how she phrased it. That made me dizzy. "It's not intuitive," she said, asking us to try again. "It takes work to blend."

My whole life sometimes seems "not intuitive." Finding the good certainly isn't. Especially at funerals. Of course, it takes work to be part of a choir. A family. A community. Why is there so much more to everything we do than meets the ear? It can take as much effort to harmonize in choir practice as it does the next morning at a library budget meeting with the mayor. But after arguing without success against a ten-percent budget cut, I want to sing so badly with the choir, to be part of a unified front, that I don't care if I am red-faced or turning blue from the effort. And I don't think it's just me.

Look at how well Nelle, who organizes the liberal "We the People" group, gets along with Barbara, whose husband blasts them in regular editorials in his conservative online newsletter. They are both second sopranos and stand right beside each other, singing the same part. Half the time they share sheet music. This is what my friend Teresa is observing when she says that community life is spiritual boot camp. Because they enjoy singing, Nelle and Barbara swallow a little pride, practice a little forgiveness, and make a lot of lovely music that transcends, for an hour a week anyway, their opposing allegiances.

Our angelic behavior did not grant us immunity from the flu that was going around, though. That was why there were only about ten of us at the next practice.

A few women were on vacations, too, taken in winter in Alaska for obvious reasons. Susie had just had her baby, so she had the best excuse.

Susie had been singing with the choir only a few weeks before her dramatic engagement a couple of years ago. She was volunteering as the host on the afternoon country music show on the public radio station when her boyfriend, Geoff, walked into the studio while she was on the air and asked her to marry him. Just like that. Live. Her microphone was on. I turned up the radio in time to hear Susie stammer, "Yes, yes!" and then clear her throat and say it was time for some more music. It was a wildly inappropriate selection, a bluegrass ballad about a Civil War hero who died drunk and alone in a muddy ditch. But she already had it cued up.

If I weren't in the choir I would have missed the response to Susie's proposal, the way we all cheered when she arrived at practice, and how Nancy led us in the John McCutcheon birthday song, improvising wedding-themed lyrics. We almost sang, "It's your wedding, we wish you many more," before Nancy loudly switched to, "It's your marriage, we wish you many years," or something like that.

The years are adding up—births and deaths, arrivals and departures, old songs and new. All held together by the strength of not one note, but so many, blending together. We will never be onstage at Carnegie Hall, but lives have been changed for the better by our music and our connection to one another through it. If I weren't in this little choir in the middle of nowhere, I wouldn't have been standing on the stage at that memorial for my good friend who died at sixty-one, singing peace with all my heart into all those tear-streaked faces. I wouldn't have truly felt Emily Dickinson's beautiful words, "Hope is the thing with feathers that perches in the soul," and better yet, because I sang about that little bird who sings sweetest in strongest gales, and never, ever, asks a crumb of me, I felt that unexpected surge of contentment.

It may sound corny, but I don't care, because it is true: Hope did perch in my soul that day and I watched it flying around that room as surely as if it were a yellow canary. Some philosophers urge young people to march to their own beat, or dance to their own music. There's a time and place for that, but I sure hope my grandchildren find a choir, and work to sing along with it. We may not be able to control when children throw up or a spouse leaves us or when one of the altos has a stroke between morning worship and the evening church potluck and won't ever be returning for the dress shoes she left by the coatrack when she pulled on her snow boots. We cannot stop a once-vigorous running companion from shrinking inside a hospital gown and disappearing entirely, but we can keep on singing. This is how we give each other a little lift on low notes, and a smile on the high ones, or share the effort in those places where staggered breathing is the only way to make it to the end of the day.

Keep on singing. This is how we
give each other a little lift on low notes,
and a smile on the high ones.

Make It Shine

By the time she died at age ninety-eight, Hilma had outlived two husbands, owned and operated the Halsingland Hotel (named for her home province in Sweden) for more than thirty years, and labored twenty more managing the adjacent Port Chilkoot Camper Park and Laundromat. My editor, Tom, whose cabin has no running water, used Hilma's public showers and washers regularly and added the word "sparkling" to my obituary copy describing her business.

Hilma kept her public showers cleaner than most private ones and even picked jars of flowers to brighten up the place in the summertime. I so admired Hilma for all her tidy, capable, and healthy Swedish ways. She was tall and lean with thick hair and she marched rather than strolled past my house on her way to the post office with her head high, taking in the little wonders of the fog thinning on the inlet, a raven cracking mussel shells by dropping them from a telephone wire onto the sidewalk, or a fisherman in a skiff trolling for king salmon.

It seemed to me that everything she did, she did well. Not because she needed to be perfect but because it made her feel good to do a good job. If Hilma was cleaning the Laundromat floor, why not make it shine? Her laundry customers would have used her washers and dryers even if the floor was gritty. Laundromats aren't that competitive around here. Her cooking, too, was simple and superb. The lilacs and roses at her hotel's entrance thrived; so did the ones scenting the humbler doorway to the Laundromat.

Hilma was a sharp businesswoman *and* she picked the berries that were in the jam she made for the hotel's breakfast biscuits (which she also baked daily from scratch). Her handwoven, decades-old hall runners still earn compliments from today's hotel guests. She set a fine table, worked all day, and then skied expertly across town in the moonlight for fun, but it was good exercise, too. On brisk mornings I would see her zooming down the hill to run errands on her Swedish kicksled.

Hilma was one of thirteen children born to poor farmers. She helped her family with the cows and her younger siblings, and worked for wealthy neighbors, weaving linens for them from flax she spun herself. She used the leftover thread to make her family washcloths. As a young woman she earned a position as cook and housekeeper at the Swedish Embassy in Washington, D.C., where she met a group of American World War II veterans who had purchased an army base outside of tiny Haines, Alaska. It overlooked a fjord, which may have reminded her of Sweden. She had married an American machinist by then, and Clarence was as game as Hilma, though he was disabled and they knew she would shoulder much of the responsibility. Off they went to the last frontier.

Hilma and Clarence transformed the vacant, once-grand commanding officer's home and another residence next door into the Halsingland Hotel; the property across the road became the Port Chilkoot Camper Park, which included the laundry and public bathrooms.

As one Alaska tourism official told me, "The Halsingland Hotel put Haines on the map back in the day; it was *the* place to stay, as quaint and quirky as it was."

The life you imagine doesn't just happen while you are daydreaming about it on the drive across the country. It requires effort once you reach your destination. Hilma and Clarence worked just about around the clock, seven days a week during the busy tourist season, making the hotel shine on all fronts. They shared a cubbyhole of a room with a bunk bed off the kitchen where Hilma cooked. Tour buses from Fairbanks would pull in at dinnertime, Hilma would make the sixty or so guests a buffet-style dinner, they'd spend one night, and in the morning she'd prepare them all breakfast before they caught their cruise ship down the Inside Passage. As soon as they vacated the rooms, Hilma and her crew stripped beds and began all over again. She was a whirlwind.

The life you imagine doesn't just happen while you are daydreaming about it on the drive across the country. It requires effort once you reach your destination.

When Hilma's oldest and dearest friend, Mary, who also once worked with her, said, "I think Hilma felt that working is what life should be, and so that is what she did," I paused. It was an ideal comment for Hilma's obituary. But I also knew that Hilma did not believe working was *all* life should be.

At least I hoped.

I called up her old friend Mary again. "Was Hilma

happy?" I asked. Mary assured me that Hilma was one of the most content women she had ever known. She was gratified by the way she lived her life.

Then she told me the best story about Hilma, and the one I want you to remember. Whenever there was a lull, and the hotel was not full, Hilma and Clarence would leave their cramped kitchen quarters and check into the best room available. She would soak in the private claw-foot tub and then they'd collapse onto sundried sheets in a full-sized bed for the night. "Hilma called it 'luxurious,'" her friend said. Her own hotel was her favorite place to stay.

Give Yourself to Love

I've decided that I'm not going to attend all the memorial services. Writing the obituary is enough. It's becoming too hard on my heart. But this one is important to the family and the community. I have to go. I don't want to be like the uncle who didn't come to my mother's service because he's "not big on funerals."

I am determined to be brave, though, and keep my distance from the sorrow. It won't be easy. She died too young of cancer, after trying every possible treatment to remain in the world she loved.

Everyone is coming down with cancer these days, it seems, even if they have taken care of themselves. A friend suggests we all may as well put more butter on our toast, since we have to die of something, and a heart attack is quick. No one lives forever. But this woman had seemed so healthy and was not yet sixty and then got lung cancer, of all things, which spread to her brain, grabbed it, and refused to let go. She was not a smoker. Her husband thinks it may be because she grew up above her mother's hairdressing shop, where they all breathed in fumes from the beauty products.

Who knows.

She was an infant and toddler expert who focused on special needs preschoolers, so there are lots of little children with her in this slide show the family has put together. That's her up on the screen, right there, the wide smile and those round eyes, petite but strong, holding her own baby girl, my daughter's classmate. That was about twenty years ago. She looks great in that swimsuit. She's glowing. She always glowed.

The family is up front somewhere, her grown son

and daughter—well, barely grown—the daughter is still in college, the son a few years older. I can't see very well over all the heads and shoulders. It's hot and both doors are open to the breeze off the cove. There's her husband. He has turned to look back at everyone. He appears to be doing okay. When I saw him at the pool once, before the cancer diagnosis, he said his wife sent him to swim laps because she was worried about his health.

Now a recording by Kate Wolf, "Give Yourself to Love," plays. "If love is what you're after," she sings, "open up your hearts to the tears and laughter." I will not cry and I definitely won't laugh. But for the family's sake I will pretend this really is a celebration of life, as the program calls it. This isn't my mother's funeral or my grandmothers' even more somber send-offs. There is no organ music. No black. This is supposed to be a party.

What a dumb idea that is.

Kate Wolf has already started to unglue me and the celebrating has barely begun. The colorful sundresses, shorts, and flip-flops make me wish it were raining and that this was a dim chapel with a few old Spanish women in mantillas and orthopedic shoes, keening, preferably in Latin. *Ave Maria.* The flashing family photos from birthdays to graduations merge with my own memories of my children and of my own dead mother. I better purge the bad haircut pictures and eighties outfits from the albums in case my family decides to produce a slide show for my funeral. But the babies, the babies I also once held, too, my own and others', who are young women and men, proof of how swiftly time passes. If I tell you these images seem like they were taken yesterday will that make me sound old? Campfires and birthday candles don't burn forever.

Stop this. No need to be morose. This was her life, not mine. And yet, we are all in this together. I can't be the only one feeling this way. Every recent death dredges up every other loss, which compounds the grief. That old hurt comes right back when I list the "survivors" in each obituary I write, and I recall friends, the former teammates in community life, acquaintances that

I never expected to outlive. Healthy, kind-spirited, active, clean-living people who did everything right have died. Oh, I have loved hard drinkers, too. The boozy karaoke singers, as well as the risk takers and ne'er-do-wells, the hotheads with hearts of gold, the friends who doubted the weather report and took off into the storm. They were the fireworks, the brilliant showers of sparks over my harbor on the Fourth of July.

All I want to do is get out of here.

Another friend, a neighbor of hers who has been asked to lead the remembrance section, stands up front, thanks us all for coming, says something sweet to the family, and encourages everyone to share good stories. He was a closer friend of the woman who died than I was and yet he is able to smile. His clear, warm gaze has a physical effect. My shoulders drop. I inhale. Okay. I will try to do as he does, and by my presence alone I'll be a comfort to the mourners. He jokes, something about there being nothing like a full house at a funeral to cheer a body up.

Oh forget it.

Who is he kidding?

Yet in rolls just and proper praise for her professional life, praise for her parenting, praise for her garden, praise for her courage and good humor in the face of death. There are pictures taken of her on tropical beaches, picking blueberries in the Alaskan rain. Kayaking. With hair. Without hair. In every one she is smiling or making a funny or thoughtful face.

This is not a funeral. It is an Event.

Won't someone release us with a dirge and an old appropriate prayer such as, "Teach us to number our days, that we apply our hearts to wisdom"? But my friend wasn't religious, though she made great potato latkes and shared them during the holidays. Why do I resist the intentional goodness here? Do I want to die a little death right now, too? Become bitter as I age? Be one of those fearful people who stays at home and watches TV rather than volunteers at the preschool with all those germs? Who won't travel to Puerto Rico with the grandchildren because the sun is too bright and I don't wear a bathing suit in public anymore?

Who doesn't make new friends because the old ones take so much less effort?

Oh, no. Now there's a video. I hear her voice again, gently teaching a little girl who has never talked how to communicate with her mother. Patiently and slowly, over the course of months, maybe a year (obviously I wasn't listening when the film began), but now in about fifteen minutes, thanks to the magic of editing, my very alive friend coaxes the child out of her shell and into the arms of her loving family. When the little girl does speak, there are tears of joy. Up on the screen and down here on my face. I swear they're on every face. I try not to sob but I can't help it.

This is why I am here.

I so admired this skilled, patient, and kind woman. She shared her joy and her knowledge of disabilities and abilities so unconditionally, without judgment. She is the one who advised me, when I was smack in the middle of a school board dispute and going nuts (and in the right, by the way), to take a "media fast." To ignore the local radio and letters to the editor in order to reconnect with the people who matter, the ones I love and who love me back.

Which brings things full circle, doesn't it?

Give yourself to love.

⌖

*You can't have love without loss.
I know that. I'm a mother, a
grandmother, and an obituary writer.
This is not my first rodeo.*

⌖

There is silent sharing all around me: A sniffle triggers a pocket search and a tissue is produced and relayed down the row. A sigh begets a hand squeeze. Slumped shoulders receive a gentle massage. Elbows touch. Eyes meet. People seated on either side of a young mother fan her fussing baby with programs featuring my friend's smiling face.

I am so ashamed for being such a jerk. I hope no one noticed.

How could I have missed what's really happening here? What was I afraid of? You can't have love without loss. I know that. I'm a mother, a grandmother, and an obituary writer. This is not my first rodeo, and even though I said I wouldn't attend another funeral unless I absolutely had to, I now know why I can't do that, and why this won't be my last, and why I will breathe a bit deeper and open my clenched heart a little wider.

Rather than lunge for the exit, I enter the circle of caring. For better or worse, I am committed, 'til we must part.

People don't gather after a death to mourn, but rather to reaffirm why life matters and to remember to exult in the only one we'll ever have. We hold funerals, memorials, celebrations—whatever you want to call them—to seek and to find the heart of the matter of this trip we call Life.

There is something divine in this old community

hall, and it is us. There's a bright, infinite "O" that transforms live into love and it's been hiding right inside of me. Time to let it out. Bring on the chanting. Bring on the prayers and songs, all of it, everywhere, and in every faith and creed and gathering of dear friends. I can't count the number of people I love, and who have died and taken a little bit of me with them, on all of my fingers and toes. That's what love costs.

And how do I possibly pay for so many blessings?

I will stand up with everyone else, any time and any place, and hold hands and sing with all my heart, soul, and mind, "This little light of mine, I'm gonna let it shine, let it shine, let it shine, let it shine."

I will make sure the goodness in you and the goodness in me meet and, what the heck, hug!

I want to leave the service hollering, "Let your light shine, people! Love one another!" Like some revival preacher. But I don't. That's not who I am, and besides, I'm wiped out. Funerals may kill me.

Instead, I will join the shuffling line to give the

family my condolences, and tell the friend who con-
ducted the service that he did a great job, her children
how sorry I am for their loss, and her husband that I'm
grateful his wife lived in our town.

She taught me to celebrate life.

Don't Judge a Lady
by Her Hat

It happened in a church with a dog in the congregation. Her name is Sissy. She's a mostly gray cattledog mix. Sissy shows up every Sunday, which is more than our priest does, through no fault of her own. The Reverend Jan Hotze is a volunteer. She has a day job as a prison counselor in Juneau, and comes home two Sundays a month when she is able. The rest of the time we lead the service ourselves.

The music is always the best part and we still have

that every Sunday. But when Nancy Nash, our pianist, announced plans to travel to Bolivia for a month, I knew we were doomed. There are only about ten of us in church on any given Sunday already, and I did not want to sit on folding chairs in a semicircle and pray. My granddaughter Caroline certainly wouldn't be able to hold still for an hour of mostly quiet reading and responses. Usually, we sit in the back. She colors and plays with the church's box of toys and jumps up when it's time to pass the collection basket, which she helps with. She sings sometimes, too, sort of randomly, but the piano and the rest of us drown out any disruption. Which brings me back to the dog. Sissy's no problem at all. She's welcome. She belongs to Granny, and they usually sit back near Caroline and me.

I'm not sure where Granny was born and reared or spent most of her life. She arrived here as an old woman with an old dog, to live in what she once told me was the only low-income senior apartment she could find that would allow her to keep Sissy. She drew stares walking through town towing a shopping cart and wearing a large red batting helmet and catcher's shin guards, always followed by her dutiful dog. I knew who she was before she sat next to us in church one Sunday, and figured it was just our luck that when we finally gained a new member, she'd be crazy. But this was church. God forgive me. The place where we are not the judge.

Caroline took to Granny right away. She was intrigued by Granny's well-stocked wire shopping cart. I whispered that she shouldn't stare. She looked harder at Granny's helmet and then the cart, and asked what was in it. Granny showed Caroline a bucket, a fishing rod (which she assembled), some extra clothes, binoculars (for bird-watching), sunglasses, dog treats, and a little box containing her false teeth. Then she put them in and smiled. She said she prefers not to wear them, as they don't fit well, but she would keep them in for church, if Caroline wanted her to. Caroline nodded yes, her eyes wide.

When Caroline tried to pet Sissy, the dog backed away. Granny told Caroline that Sissy was not used to children. She told Sissy, who had a worried look on her face as if expecting a confrontation from us, that that they were among friends and to lie down, which she did. So, we all became used to Granny and her dog and they us. Sissy even allowed gentle petting. They joined us for a church potluck at our house, and Granny and I discussed the merits of a gluten-free diet for inflamed joints, as I recall.

I was still surprised, though, when Jan announced one summer Sunday that Granny had gone to London for the Queen's coronation anniversary jubilee and the Olympics. She had left Sissy in our church's care, and members Annie and Paul had agreed to keep her until Granny returned.

There were so many questions. It didn't matter that we were right in the middle of the service and in full force, with Nancy playing piano and Jan at the altar in her white vestments, and more summer people and tourists than regulars. All pretense of formality ended. "How did Granny get to London?"

"I drove her to the ferry," Paul said.

Which does not sail all the way to England. Before I could say so, he explained that she had asked him for a ride, and that she had brought her shopping cart with her and was wearing her helmet and kneepads. Granny had also shown him her ticket from Juneau to Seattle to Heathrow.

"It was one-way," he added. "She's not sure when she'll return."

She planned to camp under bridges, and in parks and vacant lots, Jan said, reaching for her phone and thumbing through e-mails. She said Granny knew several priests at Westminster Abbey.

"No way," I heard someone whisper.

"And why wouldn't she?" someone else asked.

Jan found an e-mail from one of the priests and read us the welcoming reply.

I switched to my obituary-writing brain. That's when I search for those traits or talents that can be hidden for years, even in a small town. I love finding something out while researching a life that surprises everyone when they read the paper. I kicked myself.

I, of all people, should have known better, especially after discovering for an obituary that mild-mannered, soft-spoken sporting goods store clerk Dennis Olerud kept a vintage, polished Harley Davidson in his living room. Or that animal-loving grandma Maxine Rudd had been a World War II Marine flight instructor.

Turns out that Granny was traveling to London to volunteer to minister to the homeless while living among them, something she had done before, in many locations, apparently. She believed they would be hardest hit by all the cleaning up and special events planned because of the Jubilee and Olympics. She knew the

·····•ᚠ•·····

I, of all people, should have known better, especially after discovering for an obituary that mild-mannered, soft-spoken sporting goods store clerk Dennis Olerud kept a vintage, polished Harley Davidson in his living room.

·····•ᚠ•·····

street people would be swept out of sight. I assume, although maybe I shouldn't now that I think about it, that Granny had personal experience with that sort of crackdown. The good news is that Granny did wear her helmet, which I'm sure won't go unnoticed. We all know how the Queen feels about hats.

In the meantime, Sissy comes to church every Sunday, and I'll keep bringing Caroline as well. I want her to grow up to see beyond a person's appearance so that without prompting or proof, she'll assume the best, and discover most people have a pretty good story behind their cover.

Listen to Your Mother

"Do what you say you will.
You'd be amazed how few people actually follow through."
—SALLY VUILLET (my mother)

I had heard that Deana's mother, Ruth, had died, but I didn't call right away; it transpired just as the *Chilkat Valley News* was going to press, so her obituary would miss the deadline for that week. There is no need to make a mother's death harder on a daughter than it already is, and time helps, even if it's only a few days. I could meet Deana after my long weekend out of town.

It didn't matter to me that the ferry departure was delayed two hours while we waited for freight trucks, slowed by snow in the pass, to arrive. I had more time to visit with friends in the ship's comfortable window-lined cafeteria.

But it *was* an issue for Deana, who had a body in her minivan. It turns out that she spent those hours down in the parking lot, in line, waiting to load her car, with all that remained of her mother tucked under a quilt in the backseat. I did not know this when Deana walked into the ferry's cafeteria. I was surprised to see her traveling anywhere, even if only to Juneau, so soon after her mother's death. We embraced and she wiped her eyes. There's just no way losing your mother isn't traumatic. Every daughter I know who has gone though it struggles—the ones who have had a challenging relationship with their mothers just as much as the ones who have had a rewarding one. When our mothers die, we are on our own; there is no one to call for help, no one to blame, and no one left who has a copy of your grandmother's recipe for the traditional Christmas coffee cake, which you can't find anywhere.

Her mother's death caught Deana off guard. While Ruth had some age-related issues, the perky eighty-four-year-old had been managing fine thanks to her daughter's care, a sporty red walker, and a lifetime of physical activity. Ruth had danced with the San Francisco Ballet in her youth, which, for a girl from Casper, Wyoming, might as well have been Paris. As an adult she directed her own

When our mothers die, we are on our own; there is no one to call for help, no one to blame, and no one left who has a copy of your grandmother's recipe for the traditional Christmas coffee cake.

dance school in Wyoming. Deana had recently moved Ruth north to Alaska because her declining health had meant a lot of long visits away from home for Deana, and because Deana had recently lost some family and close friends and knew that time with her mother was precious and finite and wanted to make the most of it.

On the ferry that day, after a friend handed Deana a travel coffee mug, she sipped and smiled, and declared that gin and tonics were her favorite. More contraband cocktails were poured for the table from a thermos and we all raised our mugs when Deana toasted, "To Mom." Deana said her mother had died peacefully. She had found her in bed and at first thought she was resting.

Since there is no funeral parlor in Haines, Fireman Al and his volunteers arrived to take Ruth in the ambulance to the morgue, a chilled room adjacent to the fire hall, to await burial. Other volunteers, or the family, or a combination, would dress her for the casket. Her burial would be within three days at the town cemetery.

At least that's what usually happens.

Ruth wished to be cremated, though, and had often said so to Deana, who had promised her that she would make sure of it. "Mom was like Sam McGee," Deana said. "She had been freezing for years back in Wyoming and now in Alaska, and by God she was going to be warm when she died." The nearest crematorium is the

Alaska Mortuary in Juneau. The only way to get Ruth from here to there was by state ferry or small plane. There are no roads.

The airline required Deana to charter a flight—you can't bring a dead body on a commercial flight even if you pay for a seat. With the bereavement discount of fifteen percent, it still would have cost Deana over five hundred dollars for the forty-five-minute trip. It wasn't so much the money as the principle. Plus, Deana does not like to fly and she didn't feel right sending her mother to Juneau alone.

What about the ferry?

Fireman Al helped put Ruth on a stretcher and slide her into the back of Deana's son's minivan. Deana covered her with the quilt, a favorite one, and drove out to the terminal. They arrived an hour early and, like the rest of us, encountered the delay. That meant Deana spent a couple of hours in a pretty weird situation.

I suppose Deana could have stood in the parking lot and leaned on the hood while she waited to be waved onboard, but it was cold and rainy. Even if the weather was better, what was the right thing to do? Undertakers and ambulance drivers may be used to waiting in vehicles with bodies, but Deana had never, ever, done anything like it. And it wasn't just any corpse (not that there is such a thing, but you know what I mean), this was her mother's body. The same body that birthed her. The mortal remains of the same good mother whose spirit lives in Deana's children and grandchildren. There was a lot riding in Deana's backseat.

In the cafeteria, Deana confessed to us that, at first, when she made the decision to take the boat and they loaded Mom into the car, her adrenaline was high and it was exciting to embark on one last adventure with her mother. But when she learned the ferry would leave late, she was more than a little unnerved. What had she done? Maybe she should turn around and bury her the usual way. But she promised her mother, and she was determined to keep her word.

In the parking lot, as the minutes ticked away—ten, twenty, thirty—and turned into an hour and counting, Deana thought, *Do I pretend this is normal, and read?*

Is it okay to listen to the radio? She was so tired; a death in the family is exhausting. *What about taking a nap?*

Maybe she should keep a kind of holy silence? Or should she use the opportunity to say a few final words? Deana did tell us she caught the giggles for a second thinking of what she would tell the purser about her passenger: "No, I don't have a ticket for my mother; she's not actually here." She did have the death certificate, and reading it made tears flow. But as one hour moved into two and Deana settled in, she granted herself permission to simply be there for her mother one final time, and to be grateful that her mother had given her the confidence to do the right thing.

Deana half laughed, half cried while nursing her cocktail and sharing all this. (If anyone tries to get us in trouble for liquor on the boat, I'll swear I made this part up.) Thanks to Ruth and Deana, we all spent the rest of Ruth's last ferry ride talking about what a dutiful daughter will do, or should do, and how we know in our hearts when we are making our mothers proud, even after they are no longer able to acknowledge it.

Those of us who had already lost our mothers noted that their influence, their guidance, even their voices, remain. Deana said Ruth had been a wonderful mother. We assured Deana that she might now be an even better daughter.

I'm not sure she believed us, anymore than I would have. Maybe, like me, she thought she should have visited more in those last ten years? Or written more often back when she was in college? Or told her mother more how much she appreciated her? Is this a woman thing? That we always think we could have or should have done more?

Here's what writing a lot of obituaries of older women, with the help of the younger women who were their caregivers (by birth, marriage, or friendship), has taught me: True love is above all reliable. So we do the best we can to follow through, and that sometimes, maybe often, especially with our elderly mothers or mothers-in-law (if we are lucky enough to have family elders), we get a little frazzled and cross and want to scream; but we still wait in a doctor's office, or drive to a hair appointment, or play cards all afternoon, or drink sweetened tea when we prefer it plain, and we may think bad thoughts once in a while. And that is *okay*. Better than okay. The wisest women both here and gone have known—and demonstrated—that our actions speak loudest when it comes to love. They also know we will never regret spending this time, regardless of how we feel about it sometimes, because mothers were once daughters and that's the way life is meant to roll.

~ℓℓ~

THE NEXT WEEK, when Deana and I sat at her kitchen table to compose Ruth's obituary, she was relieved and even a little proud that she had passed a test she did not want to take. Her mother had prepared her well. Deana was at peace and much more self-assured for having granted Ruth's last wish in, she admitted, such a dramatic way. Her mother was at the table, too, in a cardboard box inside a new Bloomingdale's gift bag. "This is so perfect," Deana said, patting the package and blinking back tears, but she brightened when she told me her well-dressed mother would have been thrilled to be in the glossy "Bloomie's" bag, "in Haines, Alaska, of all places!"

I bet Ruth would have been pleased to know that when we all remember her, it will be with a smile. Because the ferry was running so late that day, one of Deana's friends feared she'd miss the last flight out of Juneau for her vacation if she had to wait for a cab to take her to the airport. She asked if it wouldn't be too much trouble for Deana to drop her off on the way to the mortuary.

"Sure," Deana said. "If you promise to keep your luggage off of Mom."

Tell Them You'll Miss Them
When They're Gone

Clyde Bell said hello to me every time he spotted me walking by, sometimes even coming out of his seafood store and crossing the street. I never said good-bye. It is hard to believe he won't be stepping out on the porch of his shop with a "How's Heather today?" and, before I can reply, telling me what I should be writing about for That Paper. "Listen, gal," he'd say, and wonder if I saw the colorful sunset last night, and what I was going to tell people about it, and didn't

I know it wasn't natural to have colored contrails or exhaust fumes behind airplanes? Those odd red and purple clouds were produced by military jets covertly spreading "chemtrails" laced with heavy metals.

Clyde believed the federal government was salting the clouds to alter the jet stream in order to change tundra into wheat-producing prairie because bread would be the new oil when everything goes to Hell Down South.

Clyde could be found most days smoking a cigarette and nursing a can of Hamm's beer at Bell's Seafood, which is in the former town jail adjacent to Bell's Store, where his wife Doris sells sundries and flowers. Bell's Seafood has a rusty potbelly woodstove by the door with a stack of firewood on the floor nearby, two aging glass-front cases—one with frozen fish, one with fresh—and some big chest freezers in the back room. The presentation is not the most beautiful, but the product is good. A lot like Clyde, actually.

He was lean, freckled, and had a boyish yet weathered face. If he wasn't at the store, there was a note on the window to see Doris next door if you needed fish. That meant he was at the harbor buying more, or cruising around town with his three-legged dog in the passenger seat of a pickup plastered with paper signs advertising his latest special: king crab legs, fresh halibut, or oysters from Prince of Wales Island.

When I heard Clyde had been medevaced to the hospital, I figured he'd be back soon. He died a day later in Anchorage. Organ failure. He was sixty. Doris said she knew Clyde was seriously ill, and so did he, but he didn't want to leave town. His brother-in-law, church elder and former volunteer fire chief Roc Ahrens, said that a few days before, Clyde had confessed he didn't think anyone would miss him.

The presentation is not the most beautiful, but the product is very good. A lot like he was, actually.

It's true that Clyde had a prickly side. But did he really not know the size of the crater his falling star would make when it finally hit the ground and flamed out?

He should have attended his memorial service at the American Legion hall. There were not enough chairs. More people stood out on the sidewalk.

One friend reminded us that when Johnny Cash died, the renter in the apartment above Clyde's store blared Cash songs out the windows for twenty-four hours. When Main Street neighbors complained, Clyde marched upstairs, turned the music even louder, and sat on the couch and listened to those songs until tears streamed down his face.

Hanging out with Clyde, another friend said, was a lot like listening to a good country song. "He was always sad and he was always laughing."

Everyone knew that when his oldest son, Matt, drowned in a swimming hole, Clyde was shattered. He'd talk about Matt's spirit visiting him from beyond. After that he connected with a lot of grieving folks. One was Steve Kroschel, who owns a wildlife park. Steve's ex-wife was killed by a caged tiger in the Lower

48. Soon Clyde was providing fish scraps to help feed Steve's Alaskan animals.

No one in Clyde's family was prepared for the size of the crowd that filled the Legion. My neighbor Elizabeth usually only attends services for close friends. When I asked her why she came, she shrugged. "Clyde was Clyde. I'll miss him." She said Clyde gave away more flowers than Doris sold. I'm sure Elizabeth had been on the receiving end. He had a soft spot for elderly widows, like her, and for parents, also like her, who had survived the death of a child.

Elizabeth wasn't the only surprise mourner. The banker paid Clyde last respects, and so did a group of kids in baggy pants who usually stand around smoking on Main Street. Proper British elder Maisie Jones was there, seated near a tank-topped, multitattooed bartender. There were pressed blouses and fishy sweatshirts. It also smelled of aftershave, tobacco smoke, diesel, sweat, shampoo, patchouli oil, and the food for the reception afterward, prepared with help from the ladies of the Port Chilkoot Bible Church.

Bar guitarist Lucky Walker took the podium last and said he had only been in town a few years, but he and Clyde had appreciated music together. He adjusted his bomber jacket, smoothed back his ponytail, set down his own guitar, held up Clyde's, and asked if an old friend of Clyde's would come up and play it. Tony, whose family owns the Pioneer Bar, walked up front wearing his best suit with a bow tie, something he said "my man Clyde" would approve of. Then Tony and Lucky played Clyde's favorite song, Ry Cooder's "Mexican Divorce," which was so out of place yet so right for the scene that it was perfectly Clyde.

In closing, Lucky and Tony led everyone in "Amazing Grace." Well, almost closing, because after that we sang "Happy Birthday" to Barbie, who waitresses at the grill half of the bar across from Bell's Store, cleans a motel, and has four young children. Lucky said, "Clyde would have wanted us to." When the song was over no one was quite ready to move to the potluck tables and instead stood around waiting for something more to happen. Lucky filled the space with "Tears in Heaven." It was the song that was played at Clyde's son's funeral. Who doesn't cry when they hear, "Would you know my name if I saw you in heaven?"

I'd know Clyde's name, and he'd know mine, and no doubt everyone else's in that hall. He'd greet us each as if no time had passed at all since he last said, "Hey gal, here's something to put in That Paper."

I don't regret not writing a column about Clyde's suspected chemtrails. But I am terribly sorry he died without knowing how much he would be missed. There aren't a lot of people who stop me on the sidewalk to share thoughts about the Great Beyond or Government Conspiracies, trusting that I'll listen. Clyde didn't know how I felt about his company, how much richer he made my life with those unusual, brief, thought-provoking chats, because I never told him, except in a "have a nice day, see you soon" kind of way.

Do the other people I care about, the ones who may not be in my inner circle but who contribute to my well-being nearly every day, not know that, either? Do yours? What should we do? Be braver, and do as the poets and saints advise—string a few kind words together, and say them out loud. It doesn't have to be a symphony or a eulogy. A country song will do. You're gonna make me lonesome when you go is plenty.

Make Your Own
Good Weather

My husband is reading a book about a man adrift in a life raft, which got us talking about being stranded on a desert island. Chip asked if I could only bring five things to eat on the island what would they be? I said, "Coffee, cream, raspberries, brown rice, and red wine." Pretty soon we were choosing what device, which author, and which musician we would need to have along to survive the ordeal emotionally. I said, "My iPhone, Mary Oliver (or maybe Emily Dickinson), and Bach."

"You never listen to classical music," Chip pointed out. "You like country songs."

"This would be an opportunity for growth," I said, thinking I should also expand my appreciation for poets beyond New England women. Then he inquired, in his logical left-brain way, how would I charge the phone?

I started to say that's not the point, this is just *pretend*; I mean, don't those smart phones have GPS tracking systems anyway? Instead, sounding snippier than I intended, I said, "Can I pack a little more and stay for six weeks?" It was almost ten p.m. and I was tired. My days and nights have been revolving around a seventeen-month-old. Our granddaughter Lani is staying with us temporarily. Her parents are in Anchorage, eight hundred miles away, waiting for her little sister to arrive. Labor began a week ago, too early, at thirty-three weeks. It has stopped now, but doctors are doing their best to keep the baby inside the womb and Stoli near the neonatal intensive care unit for at least three more weeks. (You may remember there is no hospital in Haines.) It could be longer. Term is about forty weeks.

Today, Lani's cousins, Ivy and Caroline, spent the afternoon with us. The floor is sticky and there's a playpen in the living room, a high chair in the kitchen, and I have sprained my ankle, again, stepping on a block.

The dog, Pearl, is having a grand time pulling the stuffing out of a plush moose.

It's also mid-August, one of the busiest months in Chip's busiest season. From April to September my husband's lumberyard earns our family's income for the year. So he can't help out as much as he'd like. If anyone dies right now, someone else may have to write the obituary. It's impossible to type with a child on my lap. I've tried.

But I am singing a lot. Lani thinks "Row, Row, Row Your Boat" is a fine tune. My plan is to distract her into forgetting her fear of water. She is filthy. We dug potatoes today. Lani cheered each time we found one and then she dropped it in our pail. She was so impressed by this ordinary wonder that I furtively reburied the spuds I found so she could pull them from the soil herself.

Afterward, when she refused to sit in the bathwater, even with the song, and I worried she'd slip and fall standing in the soapy tub, I stripped down and climbed in with her. To her surprise (and mine) it worked.

I had to dry and dress her first, so she wouldn't catch a cold, and before I knew how it happened, I found myself standing at the desk-turned-changing-table in the den-turned-nursery, naked. Thank God my life is not a reality TV show (even though my overarching guideline for grandchild care is, would I want their mothers to see this on videotape?). I have since hung a robe in that bathroom. I am caring for this baby with every fiber of my being, hoping that by keeping little Lani safe, healthy, and content, the sun will shine on her mother and soon-to-be sister.

We open Lani's curtains each morning and note if it is fair or stormy, clear or foggy, if the tide is high or low. I tell her there is no such thing as bad weather, thanks to our rain gear and rubber boots. We listen for the roosters and Pearl's jingling collar tags. We never watch cartoons. We stare at the drifting clouds, the waves, and the ants in the sand. We read stories. Lani won't sleep at night without *Goodnight Moon*.

The story reminds me of an obituary I wrote for a twenty-year-old who died of complications from congenital cerebral palsy. Jeremy "talked" with a voice output device, by dialing up digital recordings of sentiments he wished to express. The school superintendent recorded, "Hey, dude, step aside, I'm coming through" for him, and Jeremy replayed it as he guided his motorized wheelchair down the hallway between classes. "Despite his disabilities Jeremy had a terrific outlook on life. He was certainly a great example for all of us," Superintendent Byer told me.

When Jeremy died, his mother was so devastated that she could not speak to me. She requested that we correspond in writing for the obituary. I slipped my initial questions through her vestibule door. "How did he die?" I wrote. She wrote back, "The cat came and clawed at my bed. I woke up out of a dream in which I was reading *Goodnight Moon* to Jeremy. Got up, stoked the woodstove, went to check on Jeremy. He had just departed."

· · · · · · · · · · · · · · · · ▾▸· · · · · · · · · · · · · · · · ·

There is a reason the band continued to play as the Titanic *sank, and I think it has been much maligned. I'm going down with the horn section swinging when my time is up.*

· · · · · · · · · · · · · · · · ▴▸· · · · · · · · · · · · · · · · ·

Goodnight moon, and sun and stars.

My last note from Cherri about Jeremy arrived after the obituary had been published. She thanked me for exchanging notes the past week or so. "Heather, you are a part of this, too." She wrote "this" but I read "Life. Love. Loss. Us."

This is why I insist on finding the good: because I know some truths, which have been shared with me by people at their most vulnerable, when their hearts are so exposed and raw that it takes all their energy to compose a few lines and pass a note under a closed door into my waiting hand. As an obituary writer, it's my job to be part of Jeremy's death and to help his mother remember her son's life. But as a human being, I know that once hands are clasped, it doesn't matter who did the reaching and who responded. The comfort is in the pressure of palm on palm, of heart to heart.

The same day our daughter Sarah and her husband announced that the child who would be called Caroline was on the way, I met with the family of a teenager who had drowned while canoeing. It was Mother's Day. The parents had split up a few months earlier and the boy's mother was moving away. The father sat on the couch holding his new girlfriend's hand. The living room was full of boxes filled with clothes and household items and sacks for the Salvation Army and the dump. Photos of the son were scattered across a table and were being selected by his sister for a poster at the memorial service.

Each time I asked a question either the father answered and the mother contradicted him or the mother answered and the father said no, that wasn't correct. I don't think they even agreed on his date of birth. My questions became shorter, their answers briefer. Then it was quiet. I'd only been there about twenty minutes, but I stood up to leave, saying I was so sorry, again. That's when a silver-haired old woman came from the kitchen with mugs of tea and a plate of cookies and insisted I stay.

Everyone sipped and crunched. Then the old woman said the boy had played the piano. That he had a dog. And his parents nodded and wept, and remembered enough to fill an obituary.

This is what I do.

~ell~

ROCKING LANI BACK TO sleep at two a.m., I feel her heart beating against mine, recall my own babies' snuffling warmth, and am hit by a blue wave. The undertow of time is strong. I will never float this way again. Neither will any of us. It's not make-believe at all, is it?

So what do you plan to take on your one-way trip to

the desert island? Who do you want rowing with you in that life raft? I know I don't want to be cast away with someone who talks all day long about the hazards of falling overboard, eating raw fish, and skin cancer. Who asks, "Why didn't you pack sunscreen instead of red wine?" That will not be helpful. There is a reason the band continued to play as the *Titanic* sank, and I think it has been much maligned. I'm going down with the horn section swinging when my time is up. Also, I've decided that wherever I'm going from here, I'd rather not be in an open raft on an endless sea, even with plenty of coffee and raspberries.

Is it okay if I change the raft to my grandmother's dreamboat of a vintage Chrysler? There are wide bench seats, along with plenty of legroom and an AM radio with the baseball game on. I've already got the window rolled down and I'm pointing out all the good things I can see from here. And I'm not driving. Something bigger than me is steering this rig. Pearl is on the floor with her soft head in a grandchild's lap. I'm wedged in the back, too, amid the car seats, singing about the

Big Rock Candy Mountain, changing "cigarette trees" to "cinnamon trees," and just one more gray hair away from ditching my baseball cap and backpack and buying a wide-brimmed red straw hat and matching alligator bag, which I will stock with dog and teething biscuits, bright shiny objects of distraction, curiously strong peppermints, and a huge first-aid kit.

If I were to die tomorrow, would my grandchildren recall anything I've shown them about love and happiness? Would they even know what "find the good" means? They're too young for me to explain that yet, but I wonder if somewhere inside their brand-new silly-putty hearts there's an imprint of what I wish for them that will endure? Maybe that's a lot to ask.

It's plenty good that one loves the stars in the night sky. The other pulls open the curtains and greets the day as soon as she wakes, and a third has learned to unlatch the gate and run ahead of me to the ocean. Even if they won't recall one funny line from a story we read together or that warm egg we carried so carefully from the chicken coop to the kitchen, I bet they'll remember the fake front tooth that is our little secret. My sisters have never even seen me smile without it, but when I pop it out it makes all the grandbabies laugh, and though I wish I still had the original tooth, what's not good about that?

So I will wake early to work while the house is quiet. When baby Lani calls from her crib, I'll help her let the morning sun in, singing, "Oh, what a beautiful morning. Oh, what a beautiful day." I will change her diaper and find a dress her mother packed for her. "It's just you and me, kid," I'll say, as I pin back her curly black hair. (And to the dog: "Out of the diaper pail!")

Looking for the good may be part nature, but it can be nurtured. I believe that with my whole heart. I have learned it by writing obituaries, raising a family, and living in a small town.

Find the good, praise the good, and do good, because you are still able to and because what moves your heart will remain long after you are gone and turn up in the most unexpected places, maybe even clutched tightly in the dirty little hand of a child running along an Alaskan beach. Everyone has heard of hearts turning to stone. But stones can turn into hearts, too. I know, because I've gratefully accepted those heart-shaped rocks, dusted them off, put them in my pocket, and carried them home.

Acknowledgments

I have so many people who helped me "find the good" in this little book that I should write one thanking them. In the meantime, I'd like to acknowledge the efforts and expertise of my agent, Elizabeth Wales, and faithful Algonquin editor, Amy Gash, with deepest gratitude for your patience, wisdom, and good humor; editors past and present Elizabeth Mayhew, Ellen Breslau, George Bryson, Tom Morphet, Nancy Nash, and Liz Heywood; readers and support crew Beth MacCready, Sarah Elliott, Betty Holgate, Nancy Schnabel, Fran Tuenge, Dr. Marnie Hartman, Melina Shields, Teresa Hura, and James Alborough; and, as always, my children (and now their families)—but above all Chip, who makes life very good.